BRANDING YOUR PRACTICE

A COMPREHENSIVE GUIDE TO BUILDING A STRONG BRAND IN HEALTH & WELLNESS

Alice Pettey, MFA

NDS

NDS ENTERPRISES LLC

MIDLOTHIAN, VIRGINIA

BRANDING YOUR PRACTICE:
A Comprehensive Guide to Building
a Strong Brand in Health & Wellness
©2023 Alice Pettey

First published 2023. NDS Enterprises LLC. Midlothian, VA.

Library of Congress Control Number: 2023910869

Paperback ISBN: 979-8-9885201-0-8

ePub ISBN: 979-8-9885201-1-5

Kindle ISBN: 979-8-9885201-2-2

DISCLAIMER AND/OR LEGAL NOTICES

Preface

THE IMPORTANCE OF BRANDING IN HEALTH CARE

As a health care professional, you know how important it is to provide quality care to your patients. But have you considered the impact that branding can have on your practice? In today's competitive health care industry, branding is more important than ever. It can help you differentiate yourself from your competitors, attract new patients, and build a strong reputation.

We will explore the importance of branding in health care and why it's essential to your practice's success. You'll learn how branding can help you create a consistent and memorable image for your practice and how it can help you connect with your patients on a deeper level.

OVERVIEW

In addition to discussing the importance of branding, this book will provide you with a comprehensive guide to creating and managing a strong brand for your health care practice. We'll cover the basics of branding, including how to develop a clear brand identity, understand your target audience, and create a strong brand message.

We'll also delve into the intricacies of internal and external branding. You'll learn how to build a strong company culture that aligns with your brand values and how to manage your brand's external perception to ensure that it accurately reflects your practice's mission and values.

Throughout the book, we'll use real-life case studies and examples to illustrate how branding can impact a health care practice's reputation and bottom line. We'll also discuss the role of brand management, including how to measure the success of your branding efforts and how to adapt to changes in the industry.

By the end of this book, you'll have the knowledge and tools to build a strong brand for your health care practice. Whether you're just starting out or looking to rebrand an existing practice, this book will provide you with what need to move your practice to the next level.

Table of Contents

Preface iii

Introduction 1

PART 1: BRANDING BENEFITS AND INVESTMENT

CHAPTER 1. 5

Who's Nurturing Your Brand?

Social Media's Influence. 5

Harnessing Social Media for Practice Benefits 5

The Realm of Review Sites 6

Unearthing Employment Site Insights. 6

Exploring Professional Rating Platforms 6

Understanding Your Brand's Perception. 7

Active Brand Management is Essential. 7

CHAPTER 2. 9

The Role of Branding in Enhancing Your Practice

Differentiation: 9

Credibility and Trust: 10

Recognition: 11

Patient Loyalty 13

Premium Perception. 15

Consistency 16

Marketing and Promotion 18

Aligning Your Practice Beliefs. 19

Branding Resonance. 20

Understanding Branding is Crucial for Your Practice 21

CHAPTER 3. 23

What Resources Will I Need To Commit To Branding My Practice?

Setting a Realistic Budget 23

Developing a Comprehensive Brand Strategy 24

Leveraging Branding Expertise 24
Internal Commitment: Your Team as Brand Ambassadors 25

PART 2: FOUNDATIONS OF BRANDING

CHAPTER 4..29

What is Branding?

Isn't my logo my brand?.................................. 30
Elements of branding 32

CHAPTER 5..35

Crafting a Winning brand Strategy

Brand Purpose: Beyond Profits, a Meaningful Connection 35
Brand Vision: Painting the Picture of Future Success.......... 35
Brand Mission: Guiding Purpose into Action 36
Target Audience: Unveiling the Faces Behind the Brand 37

CHAPTER 6..39

Unleashing the Power of Internal Branding

Brand Training: Equipping Employees for Brand Success 39
Brand Communication: Guiding Employees with a Clear Vision.. 40
Brand Culture: Nurturing a Culture of Brand Excellence........ 40
Brand Engagement: Empowering Employees as Co-creators ... 41
Brand Advocacy: Unleashing the Power of Employee Voice 41
Brand Alignment: Consistency as the Key 41

CHAPTER 7..43

The Art of Brand Positioning: Carving Your Distinctive Niche

Target Audience: The Compass Guiding Your Brand........... 43
Competitive Analysis: Setting Yourself Apart................. 43
Unique Value Proposition: The Key to Distinction 44
Brand Attributes: Crafting a Distinct Identity 44
Brand Promise: The Bridge of Trust 45
Brand Personality: Forging Emotional Connections 45
Brand Messaging: The Harmonious Symphony............... 45

CHAPTER 8 47

The Art of Brand Expression: Making Your Brand Speak

Brand Identity: The Visual Symphony 47
Brand Voice: The Harmonious Melody 47
Brand Messaging: The Storyteller's Thread 48
Brand Experience: The Embrace of Connection 48
Brand Assets: The Visual Storytellers 49
Brand Culture: The Essence Within 49

CHAPTER 9 51

Power of Brand Character: Unleashing Your Brand's Persona

Breathing Life Into Your Brand: The Essence of Personality 51
Crafting a Memorable Experience: The Art of Connection 51
Aligning with Your Audience: Speaking Their Language 52
Consistency is Key: The Thread of Trust 52
Evolving and Adapting: The Dynamic Persona 53

CHAPTER 10 55

The Art of Verbal Expression: Crafting Your Brand's Voice

Crafting Powerful Messages: The Magic of Brand Messaging . . . 55
Setting the Right Tone: The Symphony of Words 55
The Language of Connection: Crafting the Right Style 56
The Power of a Name: Brand Name and Tagline 56
Captivating with Words: Content and Copywriting 57
Unleashing the Power of Stories: Brand Storytelling 57

CHAPTER 11 59

The Art of Visual Expression: Creating a Lasting Impression

The Emblem of Identity: The Power of a Logo 59
The Language of Colors: Creating Emotional Connections 59
The Art of Typography: Conveying Tone and Style 60
Visual Storytelling: The Power of Imagery 60
The Blueprint of Consistency: Visual Guidelines 61

Crafting the Visual Symphony: The Design Style...............61

CHAPTER 12...63
Reputation Management: Building Trust and Shaping Perceptions
The Essence of Reputation: A Valuable Asset 63
Listening and Shaping: The Power of Perception 63
Patient Experience: The Heart of Reputation 64
Navigating Challenges: Crisis Management.....................64
Cultivating Brand Advocacy: The Power of Engagement........65
The Digital Landscape: Online Reputation Management 65

CHAPTER 13...67
Defining Your Brand
Purpose...67
Vision..69
Mission 69
Values 69

CHAPTER 14...71
Our Employees: Do They Understand Our Brand?

CHAPTER 15...73
Who Are Our Competitors?
Your Differentiation..75

CHAPTER 16...77
Understanding Your Patients: Uncovering Insights for Effective Branding
Conducting a Brand Audit 77
Asking the Right Questions 77
Understanding the Emotional Connection 78
Developing Buyer Personas 78
Reaching Your Target Audience 79
Understanding User Intent for SEO 82
Sharing Relevant Content from Other Brands................83
Emphasizing Consistency and Effective Messaging...........84

PART 3: CREATING YOUR BRAND

CHAPTER 17. 87

Sculpting An Identity

Practice Name: A Reflection of Your Essence 87

Logo and Colors: Visual Representation of Your Essence 88

SWOT Chart: Evaluating Your Strengths, Weaknesses,
Opportunities, and Threats 89

Goals, Mission Statement, Values: Defining Your Direction 90

Patients/Target Audience: Cultivating Meaningful Connections. . 92

Patient Experience: Designing the Ideal Encounter 94

Organizational Personality: Unveiling Your Essence 97

Organizational Voice: Harmonizing Your Communication 99

CHAPTER 18. 101

Playbook for a Unified Voice

Introduction & Background 101

Brand Identity Elements. 105

Nomenclature 108

Color. 111

Signatures / Logos 115

Typography. 119

Application Standards and Templates. 120

Resources. 123

CHAPTER 19. 125

Touchpoints

PART 4: INTERNAL BRANDING & CULTURE

CHAPTER 20. 133

Foundations for Internal Communications

The Communication Process. 133

Internal Communication Strategy 134

Company wide presentation/roll-out. 135

Reinforce the brand - continuously 136
What are Internal Communications? 136
Setting the Foundations 136
Skills for Internal Communicators 137
Determining the structure of your internal communication
team. 138
Building Your Internal Communication Strategy 139
Define S.M.A.R.T. goals. 140
Define Your KPIs (Key Performance Indicators) 140
Assess the Audience. 142
Prepare a Communication Content Strategy 143
Organizational Communication Categories: 144
Create Specific Campaigns 147
Determining the Right Channels for Communication 149
Measure, Analyze, Improve 150
Infographics 151
Employee Onboarding 153

CHAPTER 21. 159

COMPANY CULTURE

The Elements of Culture: 159
Interplay of elements 170
Changing Culture. 178

PART 5: SOCIAL & REPUTATION MANAGEMENT

CHAPTER 22. 183

Outward Exposure

What is Outward Exposure? 183
Importance of Standard Operating Procedures (SOPs) in
Relation to Brand Consistency 184
Essential Branding Assets. 186
Conclusion 193
Additional Resources 193

CHAPTER 23. 197

Maximizing Your Brand's Digital Footprint

Embody Your Brand Identity:. 197
Seamless Navigation is Key:. 197
Champion Accessibility:. 198
Optimize for Mobile: 198
Content Freshness Matters: 199
Encourage Interaction: 199
Cultivate Subscribers: 200

CHAPTER 24. 201

Plan an Effective Social Media Marketing Strategy

Define Your Brand Objectives:. 201
Striking the Right Chord: Balancing Education and
Entertainment 201
Staying Current: Navigating the Fluid Digital Landscape for
Health and Wellness Brands. 203
Engagement Over Promotion: Cultivating Genuine
Conversations on Social Media. 205
Quality Over Quantity: The Essence of Meaningful Brand
Communication 207
Crisis Management in the Social Media Era. 209
Professional Management: The Key to Streamlined Social
Media Presence 210
Diverse Content: Crafting a Rich and Varied Digital Tapestry . . .212
Select Platforms Judiciously: Navigating the Social Media
Landscape with Precision 214

PART 6: REFERENCES & RESOURCES

Alice Pettey: About the Author 219
Where Does The Story Start? 219
A Shift In Focus And Change In Priorities. 220
Focus And Strategy For The Future 221

Special Offers 223

Appendices. 225

   Appendix A: Target Audience Persona Worksheet 225

   Appendix B: Elements of Branding. 226

   Appendix C: Typography Websites 228

   Appendix D: Types of Internal Communication 229

   Appendix E: Employee Communication Survey Questions 232

   Appendix F: Monthly Content Calendar. 234

   Appendix G: Content/Marketing Calendar 236

   Appendix H: Competitor Bulls Eye Diagram 237

   Appendix I: Top Competitors 238

   Appendix J: How Is Your Brand Unique? 239

   Appendix K: Brand Style Attribute Scale. 240

   Appendix L: SWOT Matrix. 241

   Appendix M: 210 Brand Attribute Terms. 242

   Appendix N: Brand Attribute Worksheet 244

Bibliography. 245

Index 249

Introduction

First off, I want to be completely honest.

This book claims to be "*A Comprehensive Guide to Building a Strong Brand in Health Care.*" It's not. Not because I don't want it to be or that I have not endeavored to make it so, it's just simply the fact. I don't know everything and even researching and compiling everything I could find, I'm certain that there are pieces that I've missed. New theories have been developed and new approaches implement. So, I wanted to be up front about it.

What you hold in your hand is my curated guidance and understanding after more than two decades of experience and continuous study in the fields of design and communication; over fifteen years of experience and expertise gained in branding and strategy; and over a decade of working with practitioners across a variety of caring professions.

With the daily evolution of technology and the ever-changing best practices in branding, marketing, and sales it's impossible to have a book that stays on the cutting edge. So, while I may not have every aspect included in this book, I do hope you will find the information within...

- detailed enough to provide you with the foundation you need,
- clear enough to prevent confusion, and
- direct enough in its actionable steps that you will see the means to brand and grow your practice.

Thank you for picking up *Branding Your Practice*. I know there are many other books out there that profess to have the key to unlocking amazing wealth from your practice. I am honored and humbled that you have picked up mine.

I am not going to promise that in six months your practice is going to be completely different. I can, however, state with assurance that if you implement the techniques covered in the following pages, you will develop a brand that stands apart from your competitors. You will connect more authentically with your desired clientele. And you will be in the driver's seat – guiding and directing where that brand is going to take your practice. Branding is a marathon, not a sprint. The returns on your investment will come, it just takes time to build. As I'm sure you understand from marketing and sales, multiple exposures are required before a sale is made. With branding we're making sure all those exposures say, feel, and emote the same way – consistent and stable.

Okay, I'm going to stop myself or I'll end up putting the whole book in the intro and that just doesn't help anyone looking for structure.

See you inside!

Alice Pettey

PART 1

BRANDING BENEFITS AND INVESTMENT

"Your brand is the single most important investment you can make in your business."

– Steve Forbes,
editor-in-chief of Forbes

Steve Forbes is an American publishing executive and businessman. He is the editor-in-chief of Forbes, a well-known and influential business magazine founded by his grandfather, B.C. Forbes. Steve Forbes is also a renowned commentator, author, and political figure.

As editor-in-chief of Forbes, Steve Forbes has played a significant role in shaping the magazine's coverage and editorial direction, focusing on business, finance, technology, and entrepreneurship. He has authored several books on economics and business, including "How Capitalism Will Save Us: Why Free People and Free Markets Are the Best Answer in Today's Economy" and "Reviving America: How Repealing Obamacare, Replacing the Tax Code, and Reforming The Fed Will Restore Hope and Prosperity."

Chapter 1

WHO'S NURTURING YOUR BRAND?

The words of branding pioneer Marty Neumeier resonate deeply with me: "Your brand is not what you say it is, but what THEY say it is." Keeping this in mind, our first order of business is understanding what people are saying about your practice and brand, as well as identifying who is voicing these opinions.

To embark on this journey, we will explore mentions of your practice across various platforms. While your own website, social media, press releases, and publications provide valuable insights, we must venture further into the realm of social media sites, review platforms, and any other corners where the public, prospects, patients/clients, or even past and current employees might have shared their thoughts about your practice.

Social Media's Influence

It is crucial to recognize the significant impact of social media in shaping the reputation of individuals and businesses alike. This fast-paced and ever-evolving landscape demands constant vigilance to stay abreast of comments and reactions.

Social media has transformed into a gatekeeper of information, superseding traditional news outlets as the primary source for many individuals. Serious news has taken a backseat to trending topics, viral content, and buzzworthy discussions. With the advent of a 24/7 news cycle, social media enables people to consume and contribute to news at any hour. Notably, platforms like Buzzfeed, surpassing the New York Times in visitor numbers, prioritize the viral and buzzworthy content.

Harnessing Social Media for Practice Benefits

When considering the advantages of social media for your practice, it becomes evident that it fosters trust and cultivates brand loyalty among your patients/clients. It serves as a convenient means of staying connected with your customer base, humanizing your brand, and reaching new, highly targeted potential customers. Additionally, it provides an opportunity to establish your practice as a thought leader in the eyes of your prospective patients/clients.

From the customers' perspective, social media empowers them to wield greater influence over your business and brand. Whether they are actively sharing information or engaging with your content, a single post can ripple across the globe in a matter of minutes. Anticipating the next viral sensation, whether it highlights your practice positively or features a disgruntled individual's critique, underscores the challenge of exerting control once a post permeates the realm of social media.

The Realm of Review Sites

While you may have reviews on your website or Google My Business account, they likely don't encompass the full extent of your online reviews. Have you considered platforms like Yelp? You may discover your practice listed on review sites you haven't even registered with, where patients/clients have been sharing their experiences without your knowledge. Occasionally searching for your practice online is a prudent move. Note: Browsers tend to personalize search results based on browsing history, so conducting the search on an alternative device or using private browsing mode can yield more unbiased results.

Unearthing Employment Site Insights

Checking your practice's reputation on employment sites can yield valuable information. Exploring platforms like Glassdoor or Indeed to see what current or former employees have shared about their experiences could prove enlightening.

Exploring Professional Rating Platforms

Regardless of your specialty, there is likely a "rate my" site available for online feedback. Whether you are in the medical field, education, or any other industry, it's worth exploring these platforms to gauge your professional reputation.

Understanding Your Brand's Perception

By examining these various channels, you gain a better understanding of how your brand and reputation are perceived by the general public. If you come across negative press, whether on social media or in reviews, it is crucial to have a plan in place to respond swiftly and mitigate the situation. Your interactions with negative comments showcase an engaged and attentive practice that acknowledges that sometimes things can go wrong. Demonstrating your commitment to rectify issues builds confidence in your practice. However, remember that social media magnifies the impact of your actions. Failing to deliver on promises will be publicly posted. Additionally, the timeliness of your responses matters. Addressing a negative comment two months later lacks the impact of a prompt reply on the same day.

Active Brand Management is Essential

It is commonly said that if your business isn't managing its brand, no one else will. While I beg to differ, it is imperative that you take an active role in brand management. Understanding your practice's essence and what it represents—its goals, values, mission statement, and unique attributes—forms the foundation. Armed with this clarity, you can develop a comprehensive strategy for brand management. This may involve establishing a robust social media presence, crafting a content marketing plan, and diligently monitoring your online reputation. Remember, this is an ongoing endeavor, requiring you to maintain a finger on the pulse of your business's reputation. Setting up Google alerts related to your practice can facilitate this monitoring process, delivering timely notifications directly to your inbox for swift action.

CHAPTER 2

THE ROLE OF BRANDING IN ENHANCING YOUR PRACTICE

Branding, a multifaceted concept, holds the potential to bring numerous advantages to your practice. Let us delve into some of the key ways branding can benefit you:

Differentiation:

In the fiercely competitive landscape of the market, branding acts as your beacon, distinguishing your practice from the multitude of similar ones. By crafting a well-defined brand, you create a unique identity that sets you apart from your competitors. The art of differentiation in branding and marketing lies in accentuating the exceptional attributes, features, or value propositions that make your brand or business stand out. This process involves skillfully highlighting the reasons why potential patients or clients should choose your practice over others.

In a competitive marketplace, differentiation serves as the linchpin of success. It enables your brand to capture attention, stand out, and leave an indelible mark on the minds of your target audience. To achieve this, it is crucial to identify and effectively communicate your unique selling propositions (USPs). These USPs, be they related to product or service features, quality, pricing, patient service, convenience, innovation, or any other pertinent factor, confer value to your target audience.

By employing differentiation strategies, you can establish a formidable competitive advantage, attract and retain patients, foster brand loyalty, and ultimately propel your practice to resounding success. Achieving this calls for an intricate understanding of your target market, competitors, and the needs of your patients. Moreover, you must artfully articulate your brand's unique value proposition. It is vital to reflect this differentiation throughout your brand positioning, messaging, visual identity, and overarching brand strategy. Consistently communicating these differentiating factors across all touchpoints cultivates a harmonious and compelling brand image in the minds of your audience.

Credibility and Trust:

A robust brand bolsters the credibility and trustworthiness of your practice. A professional and consistent brand image instills confidence in potential patients, assuring them of your practice's reliability and sterling reputation. An established brand further fosters a positive perception of your practice's expertise, experience, and service quality.

Brand credibility pertains to the perception of trustworthiness, reliability, and legitimacy a brand evokes in the eyes of its target audience. It encapsulates the degree to which patients, stakeholders, and the general public regard a brand as credible, authentic, and believable.

Building brand credibility is crucial for nurturing enduring relationships with patients, as it directly influences their trust, loyalty, and willingness to engage with your brand. Credibility is earned over time through the consistent delivery of promises, surpassing patient expectations, and maintaining an untarnished reputation.

Several factors contribute to brand credibility, including:

1. **Quality and Reliability:** Consistently delivering high-quality products, services, and experiences that meet or exceed patient expectations augments brand credibility. Brands that consistently fulfill their promises and offer reliable and trustworthy offerings are more likely to be perceived as credible.

2. **Transparency and Authenticity:** Exuding transparency and authenticity in brand communications, actions, and values contributes to brand credibility. Brands that are honest, open, and transparent in their interactions with patients, stakeholders, and the public are more likely to be perceived as credible.

3. **Reputation and Trustworthiness:** A positive reputation and a track record of trustworthiness, integrity, and ethical conduct heighten brand credibility. Brands that enjoy a solid reputation among their patients, industry peers, and the wider community are more likely to be trusted and perceived as credible.

4. **Expertise and Authority:** Establishing expertise and authority in a specific industry or domain bolsters brand credibility. Brands that demonstrate knowledge, expertise, and thought leadership in their field are more likely to be regarded as credible and trustworthy by their audience.

5. **Consistency and Coherence:** Consistency and coherence in brand messaging, visual identity, and overall brand strategy bolster brand credibility. Brands that boast a unified and consistent brand image, messaging, and visual elements are more likely to be perceived as credible and reliable.

6. **Customer Testimonials and Social Proof:** Positive patient testimonials, reviews, and social proof enhance brand credibility. Testimonials and reviews from satisfied patients offer evidence of a brand's credibility and reliability, especially when they are genuine and verified.

7. **Brand Associations and Endorsements:** Associations with credible partners, influencers, or industry experts contribute to brand credibility. Brand endorsements or partnerships with reputable organizations or individuals lend credibility and trustworthiness to a brand.

Establishing and maintaining brand credibility necessitate consistent efforts to meet patient expectations, honor brand promises, uphold a positive reputation, and demonstrate authenticity, expertise, and integrity. Credibility serves as a valuable asset for a brand, as it significantly influences patient trust, loyalty, engagement, and ultimately, the prosperity and growth of the brand.

Recognition:

Effective branding facilitates the creation of recognition and familiarity among your target audience. With a thoughtfully designed logo, cohesive visual elements, and a unified brand identity, your practice becomes memorable and easily recognizable. Consequently, this enhances brand recall and encourages patient referrals, as individuals are more inclined to remember and recommend a practice with a commanding brand presence.

Brand recognition encompasses the level of awareness and familiarity consumers have with a particular brand. It represents consumers' ability to identify a brand based on its visual elements, such as the logo, color scheme, typography, and other distinctive brand elements, even without explicit branding cues or the brand name.

Brand recognition assumes paramount importance in the realm of branding, as it enables a brand to stand out amidst the crowded market and etch an enduring impression in the minds of consumers. It constitutes a pivotal component of brand equity, which encompasses the overall value and perception a brand holds in the minds of patients, stakeholders, and the market as a whole.

Building strong brand recognition necessitates consistent and repeated exposure of a brand's visual elements and other brand assets across diverse touchpoints such as packaging, advertising, website, social media, signage, and other marketing and communication materials. The ultimate goal is to forge a distinctive and robust visual identity that becomes readily recognizable and synonymous with the brand.

Strong brand recognition begets a myriad of benefits, including:

1. **Increased brand recall:** Swift recognition and recall of a brand's visual elements contribute to heightened brand recall. This means that when prompted with a specific product, service, or category, consumers can readily recollect your brand. Consequently, improved brand awareness and recall foster enhanced brand consideration and preference among consumers.

2. **Competitive advantage:** Brands with formidable brand recognition enjoy a competitive edge over their counterparts. Being top-of-mind for consumers during their purchase decision-making process translates into elevated brand preference and patient loyalty. Familiarity and recognition often compel consumers to choose well-known brands over lesser-known alternatives.

3. **Brand association and trust:** Brand recognition plays a pivotal role in cultivating brand association and trust among consumers. Consistent exposure to and recognition of a brand instill familiarity and trust, as consumers perceive the brand as reliable and authentic.

4. **Brand consistency:** Constructing brand recognition necessitates maintaining consistency in visual elements and other brand assets across multiple touchpoints. This practice fosters brand consistency, a vital aspect of branding that contributes to a unified and cohesive brand image in the minds of consumers.

5. **Brand extension:** Strong brand recognition facilitates brand extension, which involves leveraging the equity of an established brand to launch new products, services, or business lines. When consumers possess a strong recognition of a brand, they tend to be more open to exploring new offerings under the same brand umbrella.

Building brand recognition requires patience, consistency, and strategic branding endeavors. It entails crafting a distinctive visual identity, consistently incorporating brand elements across various touchpoints, and reinforcing the brand through repeated exposure. Robust brand recognition contributes to improved brand awareness, preference, loyalty, and ultimately, enduring business success.

Patient Loyalty

Building patient loyalty is crucial for healthcare providers and organizations. When patients feel a strong connection to your practice through your brand identity, values, and messaging, they are more likely to become loyal advocates. This loyalty can result in repeat visits, positive word-of-mouth recommendations, and long-term patient relationships, ultimately contributing to the success and growth of your practice.

Patient loyalty goes beyond mere satisfaction. It encompasses the emotional bond and commitment that patients develop towards a healthcare provider or organization, leading them to choose and remain loyal over time. It is built on a foundation of trust, communication, and a deeper connection with the provider or organization.

In the healthcare industry, patient loyalty offers several benefits:

1. **Retention of patients:** Loyal patients are more inclined to continue seeking healthcare services from the same provider or organization. This leads to higher patient retention rates, a stable patient base, reduced turnover, and increased continuity of care.

2. **Increased patient referrals:** Loyal patients are more likely to refer their friends, family, and acquaintances to the same healthcare provider or organization. This word-of-mouth marketing contributes to attracting new patients, expanding the patient base, and fostering growth.

3. **Improved patient compliance:** Loyal patients are more likely to adhere to recommended treatment plans, follow-up appointments, and other healthcare recommendations. This leads to better patient outcomes, improved disease management, and increased patient satisfaction.

4. **Higher patient lifetime value:** Loyal patients tend to have a higher lifetime value as they continue to seek healthcare services from the same provider or organization over an extended period. This results in increased revenue and profitability.

5. **Brand advocacy:** Loyal patients can become brand advocates, speaking positively about their healthcare provider or

organization and promoting the brand through word-of-mouth. Brand advocacy contributes to increased brand awareness, reputation, and credibility in the healthcare industry.

To build patient loyalty, it is essential to provide high-quality patient care, establish strong patient-provider relationships based on trust and communication, deliver positive patient experiences, and consistently meet patient expectations. Effective patient engagement, personalized communication, and ongoing patient relationship management strategies are also vital in building and maintaining patient loyalty over time. Patient loyalty plays a significant role in improving patient retention, increasing patient referrals, and driving overall business success in the healthcare industry.

Premium Perception

A well-crafted brand has the power to create a premium perception of your practice, allowing you to command higher prices for your services. By establishing a strong brand presence, you can effectively convey the value and quality of your services, positioning your practice as a premium option in the market. Patients may be willing to pay a premium for a trusted and reputable brand that aligns with their needs and preferences.

In the realm of branding and marketing, premium perception refers to the belief or image that a brand or product is of superior quality, exclusivity, and worth a higher price compared to alternatives in the market. It is the perception that a brand or product carries a premium value due to its perceived higher quality, unique features, or prestigious positioning.

Premium perception is influenced by various factors, including brand reputation, product performance, design, packaging, patient service, marketing messages, and overall brand image. Brands that successfully establish and maintain a premium perception can charge higher prices, attract discerning patients, and create a sense of aspirational value.

Brands with a premium perception focus on delivering superior quality, craftsmanship, innovation, and unique value propositions that set them apart from competitors. They invest in branding and marketing efforts that emphasize their premium attributes, such as premium materials, exceptional performance, luxury, exclusivity, and an exceptional patient experience. Premium pricing strategies are often employed to reinforce the perception of higher value and quality.

Premium perception is a powerful branding strategy as it creates a perception of prestige, desirability, and differentiation in the minds of consumers. However, it requires consistent delivery of high-quality products or services, exceptional patient experiences, and effective brand positioning and marketing to maintain and enhance the premium perception over time. It also necessitates understanding and meeting the needs, preferences, and expectations of the target market for premium products or services.

Consistency

Branding plays a vital role in maintaining consistency across all touchpoints of your practice, including your website, marketing materials, signage, and patient interactions. Consistent branding builds trust, establishes familiarity, and creates a cohesive patient experience. Patients appreciate a consistent brand presence as it conveys professionalism, reliability, and attention to detail.

Consistency, within the context of branding and marketing, refers to the quality of being uniform, reliable, and coherent in brand elements, messages, and experiences across different touchpoints and over time. It entails aligning and harmonizing all aspects of a brand, including visual elements, verbal messages, tone of voice, values, and patient interactions, to create a cohesive and unified brand image and experience.

Consistency is a fundamental principle in branding as it helps establish and reinforce brand identity, recognition, and recall. When patients consistently encounter the same brand elements, messages, and experiences across various touchpoints, it fosters familiarity, trust, and reliability. Consistency in branding also sets a brand apart from competitors, builds brand equity, and creates a strong brand image in the minds of patients.

Maintaining consistency can be achieved through various brand management practices, such as:

1. **Visual consistency:** Ensuring that the visual elements of a brand, such as the logo, color palette, typography, imagery, and overall design, are consistent across all brand touchpoints, including websites, packaging, marketing materials, social media, and other communications.

2. **Verbal consistency:** Ensuring that the verbal messages and tone of voice used in brand communications, including brand taglines, slogans, brand story, and messaging, are consistent and aligned with the brand's positioning, values, and personality.

3. **Brand guidelines:** Developing and adhering to brand guidelines that provide a set of standards and guidelines for the consistent use of brand elements, messages, and experiences across different channels, platforms, and media.

4. **Employee training:** Providing training and education to employees to ensure they understand and consistently represent the brand in their interactions with patients, suppliers, and other stakeholders.

5. **Monitoring and feedback:** Regularly monitoring and evaluating brand touchpoints, patient feedback, and market research to identify any inconsistencies or misalignments and taking corrective actions to maintain consistency.

Consistency in branding helps create a strong and memorable brand image, build patient trust and loyalty, and establish a sustainable competitive advantage in the market. It contributes to building a solid brand foundation that resonates with patients and supports long-term brand success.

Marketing and Promotion

A well-defined brand serves as the foundation for your marketing efforts. By utilizing your brand positioning, messaging, and visual elements, you can create a consistent and cohesive message throughout your marketing and promotional activities. Branding provides a framework for your marketing strategies, enabling you to effectively communicate your unique value proposition and build relationships with your target audience.

Branding, marketing, and promotions are interconnected concepts that work together to create awareness, perception, and preference for a brand or product among target audiences. Let's briefly explore each concept:

1. Branding involves creating and managing a brand's identity, image, and reputation. It encompasses defining the brand's positioning, personality, values, visual and verbal elements, and overall strategy. Branding aims to establish a unique and differentiated brand image in the minds of consumers, leading to brand recognition, recall, and loyalty. It serves as the foundation for all marketing and promotional efforts by defining the brand's essence and guiding its communication to the target audience.

2. Marketing entails promoting and selling products or services to patients. It encompasses activities such as market research, market segmentation, product development, pricing, distribution, and promotion, all aimed at creating and delivering value to patients. Marketing strategies and tactics are developed based on a deep understanding of patient needs, preferences, and behaviors and are aligned with the overall brand strategy. The goal of marketing efforts is to attract, engage, and retain patients, generate sales, and build patient relationships.

3. Promotions involve specific activities and tactics used to communicate and promote a brand or product to the target audience. This includes advertising, public relations, sales

promotions, events, social media campaigns, influencer marketing, and other promotional activities. Promotions are designed to create awareness, generate interest, stimulate demand, and drive sales. They are often aligned with the brand's messaging, visual elements, and overall identity to ensure consistency and reinforce the brand image and positioning.

Branding, marketing, and promotions work together in a holistic approach to building and promoting a brand or product. Branding sets the foundation by defining the brand's identity and strategy, marketing develops strategies and tactics to reach and engage the target audience, and promotions execute specific activities to communicate and promote the brand or product to the market. A well-coordinated and integrated approach to branding, marketing, and promotions can help create a strong brand presence, generate patient interest and loyalty, and drive business success.

Aligning Your Practice Beliefs

Branding that aligns with your practice's beliefs can have numerous benefits. Firstly, it ensures consistency and coherence throughout your brand, encompassing visual and verbal expressions, positioning, and overall strategy. This cohesive message resonates with your target audience, building trust and credibility while maintaining an authentic identity.

Secondly, aligning your branding with your beliefs sets you apart from the competition, showcasing your unique qualities. By reflecting your distinctive values, your branding establishes a special position in the market, attracting patients who share similar beliefs or connect with your brand story.

Moreover, branding aligned with your beliefs fosters an emotional connection with patients. When your branding genuinely conveys your beliefs and values, it evokes emotions and resonates with your target audience. Patients are more likely to connect with a brand that aligns with their own beliefs, leading to increased loyalty and long-term relationships.

Furthermore, this alignment cultivates brand loyalty and advocacy. Patients who identify with your brand's beliefs and values become loyal advocates, promoting your practice through word-of-mouth recommendations and positive online reviews.

Additionally, branding aligned with your beliefs contributes to an enhanced reputation and credibility. Consistently reflecting your beliefs and values creates an impression of authenticity, trustworthiness, and reliability, positively influencing your practice's reputation.

To summarize, branding aligned with your beliefs benefits your practice by establishing consistency, differentiation, emotional connection, brand loyalty, and enhancing reputation and credibility. This approach builds a strong brand identity and fosters positive relationships with patients, leading to long-term success.

Branding Resonance

When it comes to branding resonance, which refers to the emotional connection and resonance your brand creates with patients, there are several positive effects for your practice:

Firstly, branding resonance increases patient engagement. Patients connect with brands that resonate with their emotions, values, and beliefs. As a result, they become more engaged, interested, and committed to your practice.

Secondly, it enhances patient loyalty. When your brand resonates with patients, it fosters a sense of loyalty and commitment. This leads to repeat visits and long-term relationships. Emotionally connected patients are more likely to remain loyal, refer others, and become brand advocates.

Additionally, branding resonance contributes to positive patient experiences. Patients feel aligned and connected to your practice, resulting in improved satisfaction, trust, and overall experience. This leads to positive word-of-mouth referrals and online reviews.

Moreover, branding resonance differentiates your practice from competitors. Creating a unique emotional connection with patients sets you apart, as they prefer brands they resonate with over others.

Furthermore, it contributes to increased practice reputation. Branding resonance generates positive reviews, testimonials, and recommendations, enhancing your practice's reputation and credibility.

Branding resonance positively impacts your practice through increased patient engagement, enhanced loyalty, improved patient experiences, differentiation from competitors, and an enhanced reputation. It creates a strong emotional bond between your brand and patients, leading to long-term success.

Understanding Branding is Crucial for Your Practice

Understanding branding allows you to develop consistent brand messaging. By effectively communicating your practice's values, unique selling proposition, and key messages, you create brand recognition and recall. This builds a cohesive brand image in patients' minds, resulting in increased awareness and preference.

It also enables strategic brand positioning. Understanding branding helps you identify your target audience, their needs, preferences, and perceptions. Aligning your brand accordingly sets you apart from competitors, attracting the right patients and establishing a competitive edge.

Furthermore, branding understanding allows you to design a consistent and memorable brand experience. From the physical environment to online presence, patient service, and interactions, a positive and consistent brand experience improves patient satisfaction, loyalty, and advocacy.

Moreover, branding understanding helps build brand equity. This intangible value and perception associated with your brand can command higher patient loyalty.

CHAPTER 3

WHAT RESOURCES WILL I NEED TO COMMIT TO BRANDING MY PRACTICE?

Branding your practice requires a strategic allocation of resources, including time, effort, and budget. The specific resources needed depend on the scale and complexity of your branding endeavors. Here we explore the essential resources you need to consider when committing to branding your practice effectively and sustainably.

Branding like any endeavor is going to take time, expertise, and money. It's all a question of how much of each you are willing, or able to devote. Having less in one area inevitably requires more in another.

Setting a Realistic Budget

Branding efforts come with financial implications, and setting a realistic budget is crucial. The cost of branding your practice can vary significantly depending on factors such as the scope of work, the complexity of branding initiatives, and the expertise and reputation of the professionals you engage.

Consider the following common branding expenses:

a. **Brand Design and Development**: This includes the creation of your logo, visual elements, and brand guidelines. The cost will depend on factors such as design complexity, revisions, and the experience of the designer or agency you choose to work with.

b. **Website Development**: Establishing a professional website that reflects your brand can be a significant expense. Factors such as features, functionality, design, and development complexity will influence the cost.

c. **Marketing and Promotions**: Allocating resources for advertising, social media campaigns, content creation, and other promotional activities is vital to establish brand awareness. The cost will depend on your marketing goals, target audience, chosen channels, and the scale of your promotions.

d. **Ongoing Monitoring and Management**: Branding is an ongoing
    effort that requires continuous monitoring and management.
    Allocating resources for brand monitoring, online review and
    reputation management, updating brand assets, and adapting
    your brand strategy as needed is essential for long-term
    success.

Remember that branding is not a one-time expense but an ongoing
investment. It is essential to factor in both initial costs and ongoing
maintenance to ensure consistent and effective branding

Developing a Comprehensive Brand Strategy

A solid foundation for successful branding begins with the
development of a comprehensive brand strategy. This entails
investing time and effort to define your brand's values, positioning,
and messaging. By clearly understanding your brand's identity and
target audience, you can shape a strategy that resonates with your
patients and differentiates you from competitors.

Crafting a brand strategy often benefits from the expertise of
branding professionals or agencies. Their insights and experience
can guide you in conducting brand research, competitor analysis, and
defining a strategic roadmap for your brand's success.

Leveraging Branding Expertise

If you lack in-house branding expertise, it may be necessary to
invest in external resources like branding agencies, marketing
consultants, or graphic designers. These professionals can provide
valuable guidance and support in developing and executing your
brand strategy effectively.

Consider the following areas where external expertise can be
beneficial:

a. **Brand Strategy and Research**: Collaborate with branding
    agencies or consultants to conduct brand research, competitor

analysis, and develop a comprehensive brand strategy that aligns with your practice goals. The cost will depend on the scope and expertise involved.

b. **Designing Brand Assets**: Engage experienced designers or agencies to create visually compelling brand assets, such as business cards, letterheads, signage, brochures, and marketing materials. The cost will depend on factors such as design complexity, printing methods, and production quality.

Investing in branding expertise can provide valuable insights, save time, and help you achieve a more impactful and cohesive brand presence. Brand expertise is like any other service there are levels of competency, so take your time when identifying who to work with. It's not just about skill either. It's also important that you and the expert that you are working with have a good rapport. You will be investing quite a bit of time, money and trust in this person. You need to be comfortable with them.

Internal Commitment: Your Team as Brand Ambassadors

A successful brand relies on the commitment and alignment of your entire team. Ensuring that your employees embrace your brand values and consistently represent your brand in their interactions with patients and stakeholders is crucial.

Consider the following aspects of internal commitment:

a. **Brand Training and Onboarding**: Provide brand training and onboarding sessions to ensure that your staff comprehends the brand strategy, values, messaging, and guidelines. This empowers them to embody your brand in their daily interactions.

b. **Brand Consistency and Implementation**: Foster consistency in brand representation across various touchpoints, including patient interactions, marketing materials, and digital assets. Ensure that your staff adheres to correct brand messaging, visual elements, and maintains a consistent tone of voice.

c. **Internal Brand Engagement**: Foster a positive company culture where staff members embrace and exemplify your brand values. Incorporate your brand into internal communications and activities to create a consistent brand experience for both employees and patients.

d. **Brand Monitoring and Management**: Dedicate time and effort to monitor and manage your brand's reputation, online presence, and adherence to brand guidelines. Encourage staff members to actively contribute to maintaining a positive brand image.

e. **Brand Advocacy**: Empower your staff to serve as advocates for your brand. Encourage them to share positive stories, testimonials, and experiences related to your brand. Train them to be brand ambassadors in their interactions with patients, colleagues, and other stakeholders.

Branding your practice requires a thoughtful allocation of resources. By developing a comprehensive brand strategy, setting a realistic budget, fostering internal commitment, and leveraging branding expertise when needed, you can pave the way for a successful branding outcome.

PART 2

FOUNDATIONS OF BRANDING

"Your brand isn't what you say it is. It's what they say it is."

— Marty Neumeier
Director of CEO Branding,
Liquid Agency

Marty Neumeier is a renowned expert on brand strategy and innovation, with a focus on helping businesses and individuals develop distinctive and successful brands. He has written several influential books, including "The Brand Gap," "Zag," and "The Designful Company," which have become widely recognized resources in the branding industry.

Neumeier is known for his insightful and accessible approach to branding, emphasizing the importance of differentiation, simplicity, and meaningful customer experiences.

CHAPTER 4

WHAT IS BRANDING?

Branding refers to the process of creating a unique and recognizable identity for a product, service, company, or individual. It involves developing a distinctive name, logo, tagline, design, and overall visual and verbal representation that sets apart a brand from its competitors and conveys its core values, personality, and promises to its target audience.

In healthcare, branding is crucial for practices looking to establish a strong reputation, attract new patients, and differentiate themselves from competitors. A clear brand identity can increase patient loyalty and trust, enhance a practice's reputation, and improve its bottom line. Effective branding can also help healthcare practices stay top-of-mind for patients and referral sources, ultimately leading to increased revenue and growth.

Branding is not limited to just a logo or visual elements, but it also encompasses the emotional and psychological connection that consumers have with a brand. It is not just about creating a consistent and cohesive brand experience across all touchpoints, including advertising, marketing materials, packaging, website, social media, patient service, and more.

A successful healthcare brand starts with a clear brand identity, which includes defining a brand's mission, values, and personality, as well as developing a memorable name and logo. By developing a strong brand message that resonates with patients, healthcare practices can create a powerful emotional connection with their audience. In addition to establishing a strong brand identity, healthcare practices should also focus on building a positive company culture to improve patient outcomes and build a strong reputation in the industry.

A strong brand can communicate to patients that your practice is reliable, reputable, and capable of providing the care they need. This can lead to increased patient loyalty and positive word-of-mouth referrals.

Branding can also help healthcare practices differentiate themselves from competitors. With so many options available to patients, it's important to stand out in the market. A well-crafted brand can communicate your unique selling proposition and help you capture the attention of potential patients.

Another benefit of branding in healthcare is improved patient engagement. By developing a strong brand identity, healthcare practices can create a sense of community and foster meaningful connections with patients. This can lead to increased patient satisfaction and better health outcomes.

Branding is an essential component of healthcare marketing and can have a significant impact on a practice's success. By developing a clear brand identity, understanding the benefits of branding, and studying successful healthcare brands, healthcare professionals can position themselves for long-term growth and success.

Overall, branding is a powerful tool that healthcare practices can use to build trust, differentiate from competitors, and improve patient outcomes. By investing in their brand identity and creating a positive company culture, healthcare professionals can position themselves for long-term growth and success.

Isn't my logo my brand?

No, branding is not just limited to a logo. While a logo is an important visual element of branding, branding encompasses much more than just a logo. A logo is a graphic symbol or mark that represents a brand, but branding involves the entire process of creating and managing a brand's identity, personality, and perception in the market.

A brand is a person's gut feeling about a person, product, service, or organization.

- We make our most important decisions using OUR emotions so your brand *must connect emotionally*.

- It's about answering the question **what do people think of us?**
- It's finding **what we can do that we can help them** *see us.*
- Our brand is truly what **THEY say it is**. (It must ALWAYS be seen from the patient's point of view!!)
- It's whatever the *"something"* is that your patient UNDERSTANDS about you.

Branding is your reputation, your quirkiness, your dreams, and your aspirations. It's all the little thing that makes you ... you. You personally have a brand, a business has a brand, even your dog or cat has a brand.

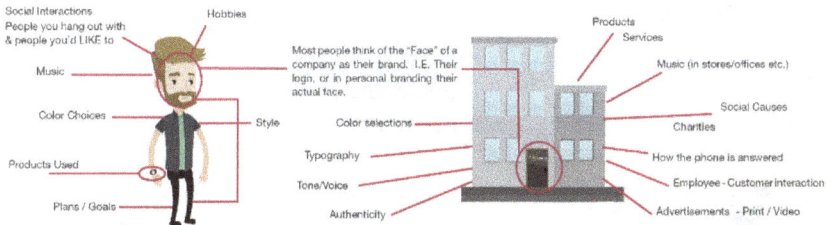

As you can see from the graphic above, the concept of a brand doesn't really matter who or what is being branded, the principles remain the same. In fact, when I work with companies on developing their business brand, I recommend that they think of their business as a person. As people, we can understand the social interactions, likes, and dislikes of our fellow humans, it's when we take that to the abstract concept of a business that we start to have problems. So, I ask that for the duration of your time going through this workbook, pretend that your business is your friend. Give it a name. It will make the process is little more natural.

Don't forget BRANDING HAPPENS whether you put anything out or not. You don't want yours to be a case of *Accidental Branding* (no reputation management) where you have had NO influence or control.

Defining your brand may seem straightforward, but beware of the trap of oversimplification. It takes more than a flashy logo to create a brand identity that resonates with your audience.

Your brand should immediately convey what your business stands for and what it offers. A tried-and-true strategy is to focus on quality and convenience, and tie your brand identity to delivering value. Your patients should associate your product or service with being top-quality, easy to use, affordable, or long-lasting.

Don't rely on hype to make an impact, as it will only take you so far. Your goal is to create a unique and appealing voice for your brand that stays with your audience long after they've left your website or put down your brochure. Your message should leave a lasting impression and make choosing your product or service the most logical decision.

Elements of branding

Branding includes various elements, such as:

1.   Brand Strategy: This involves defining the brand's purpose, vision, mission, and values. It includes understanding the target audience, competitive landscape, and market positioning.

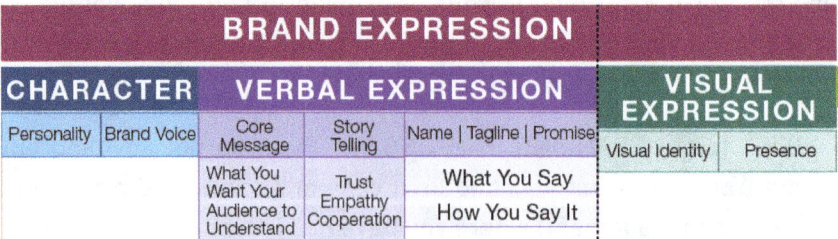

BRAND EXPRESSION						
CHARACTER		**VERBAL EXPRESSION**			**VISUAL EXPRESSION**	
Personality	Brand Voice	Core Message	Story Telling	Name | Tagline | Promise	Visual Identity	Presence
		What You Want Your Audience to Understand	Trust Empathy Cooperation	What You Say / How You Say It		

3.   Brand Messaging: This includes the verbal elements that convey the brand's voice, tone, and messaging. It includes the brand's tagline, brand story, value proposition, and key messages that communicate the brand's essence and unique selling proposition.

4.   Brand Experience: This encompasses the overall experience that patients have with a brand at every touchpoint, from advertising and marketing materials to product packaging, website, patient service, and more. It includes the emotions, perceptions, and interactions that patients associate with the brand.

5.   Brand Promise: This refers to the commitments and promises that a brand makes to its patients. It includes the brand's quality, reliability, trustworthiness, and the value it delivers to its patients.

6.   Brand Consistency: This involves maintaining a consistent brand image and message across all touchpoints to create a cohesive and unified brand presence. Consistency in branding helps to build brand recognition and trust among consumers.

A logo is an important visual representation of a brand, but it is just one element of the broader branding process. An effective branding strategy considers all these elements and creates a holistic and cohesive identity that resonates with the target audience, differentiates from competitors, and builds a strong brand reputation.

See appendices for comprehensive chart of the elements of branding.

CHAPTER 5

CRAFTING A WINNING BRAND STRATEGY

In the vast world of branding, a successful brand strategy serves as the guiding light that illuminates the path to a thriving and revered brand. It lays the foundation upon which all branding activities are built, offering a roadmap to navigate the intricate landscape of brand positioning, perception, and management. In this chapter, we will delve into the essential components of a compelling brand strategy, unveiling the secrets to building a brand that captivates hearts and minds.

Brand Purpose: Beyond Profits, a Meaningful Connection

Imagine a brand that transcends the pursuit of profits—a brand that resonates deeply with consumers, creating a profound emotional connection. This is the power of brand purpose. It goes beyond the mere existence of a brand and delves into its reason for being. Why does the brand exist? What is its greater mission in the world? These questions lie at the core of brand purpose.

Brand purpose empowers a brand to make a difference beyond its products or services. It defines the higher calling that propels the brand forward and shapes its identity and messaging. When a brand's purpose aligns with the values and aspirations of its target audience, magic happens. Consumers are drawn to the brand not just for what it offers, but for the shared values and vision it represents.

Take the example of a healthcare practice that goes beyond treating patients and aspires to transform lives through compassionate care. This purpose becomes the driving force that inspires both the healthcare professionals and the patients they serve. By weaving the brand purpose into its messaging and actions, the practice cultivates an emotional bond, fostering trust and loyalty among its patients.

Brand Vision: Painting the Picture of Future Success

Every great brand begins with a vision—an audacious dream of what the brand aspires to become in the hearts and minds of consumers. A brand vision is the compass that guides the brand's journey toward its desired future state. It paints a vivid picture of success and sets the course for growth and development.

Imagine a brand in the healthcare industry with a vision to revolutionize the way people approach preventive care. This vision propels the brand to constantly innovate, explore new horizons, and redefine industry standards. It becomes a rallying cry for the brand's team and a beacon of inspiration for its target audience.

A clear and compelling brand vision serves as a constant reminder of the destination the brand aims to reach. It fuels motivation, drives strategic decision-making, and instills a sense of purpose and direction in every aspect of the brand's operations.

Brand Mission: Guiding Purpose into Action

While brand purpose sets the stage and brand vision paints the picture, it is the brand mission that brings them to life. A brand mission articulates the brand's overall purpose and outlines what it seeks to accomplish in the short term. It reflects the brand's core activities, values, and unique value proposition.

Think of the brand mission as the strategic framework that underpins the brand's day-to-day operations and decision-making. It ensures that every action taken by the brand aligns with its purpose and vision. A well-crafted brand mission statement serves as a compass, guiding the brand through the complex landscape of opportunities and challenges.

For a healthcare practice, the mission could be centered around delivering personalized, patient-centric care that improves the overall well-being of individuals. This mission permeates every interaction, from the first phone call to the follow-up appointments, reinforcing the brand's commitment to its patients' health and happiness.

Target Audience: Unveiling the Faces Behind the Brand

Understanding the specific group(s) of consumers that a brand aims to serve and connect with is essential to successful branding. This entails delving deep into the demographic, psychographic, and behavioral characteristics of the target audience.

Imagine a healthcare brand catering to the needs of busy professionals seeking convenient and accessible healthcare solutions. By understanding the unique challenges, preferences, and aspirations of this target audience, the brand can tailor its positioning, messaging, and marketing efforts effectively. It can craft a brand experience that speaks directly to their needs, creating a lasting impression and forging a meaningful connection.

Understanding the target audience is like peering into a mirror. It allows the brand to see its reflection—the values, desires, and pain points of its consumers. This insight is invaluable in creating a brand that resonates authentically, forming an emotional bond with its intended audience.

In the next section we will break down the first of the two major areas of brand strategy - internal branding and positioning.

INTERNAL BRAND				POSITIONING	
SECONDARY CORE MESSAGE				Audience	Offering
Vision	Mission	Values	Purpose - The Why	POSITIONING STATEMENT (PRIMARY CORE MESSAGE)	
				Target Audience	Competitors	Difference

CHAPTER 6

UNLEASHING THE POWER OF INTERNAL BRANDING

In the fast-paced world of healthcare, where patient experiences and brand reputation reign supreme, there is a hidden force that can make or break a brand—internal branding. Often known as employee branding or internal marketing, internal branding is the art of aligning and engaging employees with the very essence of a brand. It goes beyond catchy slogans and flashy logos; it cultivates a brand-oriented culture within the organization, where employees are the heart and soul of the brand experience.

Recognizing the pivotal role employees play in a brand's success, internal branding weaves a tapestry that connects their daily actions to the brand's values, mission, vision, culture, and brand promise. From the moment they interact with patients to the delivery of products and services, employees become brand ambassadors, breathing life into the brand experience.

The power of internal branding lies in understanding that employees are not just stakeholders; they are the driving force behind a brand's success. When employees truly grasp, embrace, and align themselves with the brand's core values, positioning, and promise, the impact on patient satisfaction, loyalty, and brand reputation is profound.

So, how do we unleash the power of internal branding? Let's explore the key activities and initiatives that pave the way for a strong brand-oriented culture within the organization:

Brand Training: Equipping Employees for Brand Success

In the world of healthcare, knowledge is power. Brand training empowers employees by providing them with the necessary training and resources to understand the brand's identity, values, positioning, and messaging. By educating employees on how their roles contribute to the overall brand experience, they become equipped with the knowledge and skills to consistently deliver the brand promise.

Imagine a healthcare practice that invests in comprehensive brand training, ensuring that every employee, from the receptionist to the healthcare providers, understands the brand's unique identity and their role in upholding it. This training builds a solid foundation of brand knowledge and instills a sense of purpose and pride in employees, fostering a culture of excellence.

Brand Communication: Guiding Employees with a Clear Vision

Communication is the lifeblood of any successful organization. In the realm of internal branding, transparent and regular communication about the brand's vision, mission, and goals is paramount. By keeping employees informed about the brand's progress, achievements, and challenges, they remain aligned with the brand's direction and objectives.

Consider a healthcare brand that holds regular town hall meetings, where leadership shares updates on the brand's initiatives, successes, and future plans. This open dialogue creates a sense of unity and purpose among employees, enabling them to understand the bigger picture and how their individual contributions impact the brand's journey.

Brand Culture: Nurturing a Culture of Brand Excellence

A brand is more than a logo or a tagline—it is a living, breathing entity with its own personality and values. Internal branding fosters a brand-oriented culture within the organization, where the brand's values, personality, and identity permeate every aspect of the work environment.

Creating a positive work environment is essential to nurturing a brand culture. Recognition and rewards for behaviors that align with the brand's values become the norm, reinforcing the importance of upholding the brand's promise. When employees feel a sense of pride and ownership in representing the brand, they become passionate advocates, delivering exceptional experiences to patients.

Brand Engagement: Empowering Employees as Co-creators

Innovation and growth thrive in environments that encourage collaboration and engagement. Internal branding involves actively involving employees in brand-related activities and initiatives, creating opportunities for them to contribute their ideas, insights, and feedback.

Imagine a healthcare brand that organizes brand workshops and brainstorming sessions, where employees from different departments come together to share their perspectives and contribute to the brand's development. This sense of ownership and engagement fuels creativity, strengthens employee loyalty, and fosters a culture of continuous improvement.

Brand Advocacy: Unleashing the Power of Employee Voice

Employees possess a powerful voice that can amplify the brand's message far and wide. Brand advocacy involves empowering employees to be vocal advocates for the brand, both within and outside the organization. By encouraging employees to share the brand's values and messages, they become catalysts for positive change.

Consider a healthcare practice that equips its employees with the tools and resources to promote the brand on social media, in their personal networks, and even in their interactions with patients. By tapping into the collective influence of employees, the brand's reach expands exponentially, creating a ripple effect of trust and loyalty.

Brand Alignment: Consistency as the Key

Consistency is the secret ingredient that brings a brand's vision to life. Internal branding ensures that all internal processes, policies, and behaviors are aligned with the brand's values and promise. From actions to decisions, employees become custodians of the brand, ensuring that every touchpoint reflects the brand's positioning and messaging.

Imagine a healthcare organization where every employee, from the janitor to the CEO, understands and embodies the brand's values, consistently delivering experiences that align with the brand promise. This harmonious alignment creates a cohesive brand identity that resonates with patients, forging enduring connections and building a robust brand reputation.

Internal branding is the thread that weaves together the fabric of a strong brand culture. By empowering employees to understand, embrace, and live the brand's values, positioning, and promise, internal branding sets the stage for consistent brand delivery, improved patient experiences, and a brand reputation that stands tall.

Stay tuned, as we embark on an exciting journey into the realm of brand positioning. Together, we'll uncover the strategies and insights that will differentiate your brand from competitors and create a lasting impact in the minds of your target audience. Join us as we unveil the secrets to crafting a compelling brand positioning that sets your brand apart.

CHAPTER 7

THE ART OF BRAND POSITIONING: CARVING YOUR DISTINCTIVE NICHE

Imagine strolling through a bustling marketplace, where numerous brands compete for your attention. In this sea of choices, one brand manages to capture your imagination, standing out like a shining beacon. This phenomenon is none other than brand positioning—a strategic process that carves a unique and distinctive place for a brand in the minds of consumers.

Brand positioning is not merely about finding any spot in the crowded marketplace; it's about claiming the perfect spot that resonates with your target audience. It's about crafting a perception and image that captures the hearts and minds of consumers, based on their beliefs, experiences, and interactions with your brand.

To understand the power of brand positioning, let's explore the elements that contribute to its success:

Target Audience: The Compass Guiding Your Brand

Every brand needs a true north—a specific group of consumers it aims to serve. Understanding the needs, preferences, and behaviors of your target audience is essential for tailoring your brand positioning to resonate with them. Think of it as a compass guiding your brand towards the hearts of those who matter most.

Consider a health supplement brand that targets health-conscious millennials seeking natural and sustainable solutions. By intimately understanding this audience's desires for holistic well-being and eco-friendly choices, the brand can position itself as the go-to choice, speaking directly to their aspirations and needs.

Competitive Analysis: Setting Yourself Apart

The marketplace is a battlefield, and brands are constantly vying for attention. To claim your position, a thorough analysis of your competitors is crucial. Assess their strengths and weaknesses, identifying opportunities for differentiation. This enables you to strategically position your brand in a unique and compelling way, setting it apart from the competition.

Imagine a dental clinic in a city saturated with similar practices. By conducting a comprehensive competitive analysis, the clinic discovers a gap—a lack of personalized, patient-centered care. They seize this opportunity, positioning themselves as the trusted, compassionate dental practice that goes the extra mile to ensure patient comfort and satisfaction.

Unique Value Proposition: The Key to Distinction

What sets your brand apart from the rest? Your unique value proposition holds the answer. Define the exceptional value your brand offers to consumers and how it solves their problems or fulfills their needs better than competitors. This forms the foundation of your brand's positioning and acts as a beacon for your target audience.

Think of a telehealth platform that revolutionizes access to healthcare. Its unique value proposition lies in its ability to provide instant virtual consultations with renowned specialists, eradicating the barriers of distance and wait times. By highlighting this advantage, the brand positions itself as a game-changer, connecting patients to top-tier healthcare expertise at their fingertips.

Brand Attributes: Crafting a Distinct Identity

Your brand possesses a unique set of attributes that make it memorable and appealing to your target audience. These attributes, carefully identified and nurtured, differentiate your brand from the competition. They encompass qualities such as quality, reliability, innovation, affordability, sustainability, and more.

Consider a skincare brand that prides itself on using organic and cruelty-free ingredients. By highlighting these attributes, the brand positions itself as a conscious, trustworthy choice for consumers who value ethical and sustainable practices. This distinctive identity becomes an integral part of the brand's positioning strategy.

Brand Promise: The Bridge of Trust

Every successful brand makes a promise—a commitment to deliver a specific benefit or value to consumers. This promise acts as a bridge of trust, setting the expectation and perception of your brand in the minds of consumers. A well-crafted brand promise creates anticipation and builds a loyal following.

Imagine a wellness retreat that promises an immersive experience of rejuvenation and self-discovery. By articulating this promise, they position themselves as the ultimate destination for those seeking holistic wellness, drawing in individuals who yearn for a transformative escape from the demands of daily life.

Brand Personality: Forging Emotional Connections

Humanizing your brand can forge deeper emotional connections with your target audience. Define the human-like characteristics, traits, and qualities that align with your brand's identity. This not only creates relatability but also influences how consumers perceive and engage with your brand.

Think of a fitness apparel brand that embodies energy, motivation, and resilience. By infusing their brand personality with these attributes, they connect with fitness enthusiasts on a personal level, inspiring them to push their limits and embrace an active lifestyle. The brand becomes more than just clothing; it becomes a symbol of empowerment.

Brand Messaging: The Harmonious Symphony

Crafting clear and consistent messaging is vital in communicating your brand's positioning, value proposition, and promise to consumers. Your brand message should resonate through various touchpoints, from advertising and marketing materials to your website, social media platforms, and even patient interactions. It is the harmonious symphony that amplifies your brand's voice.

Consider a healthcare organization that consistently communicates its patient-centric approach through empathetic language and compelling stories of transformative healing journeys. This brand messaging reinforces its positioning as a compassionate ally, connecting deeply with patients seeking both medical expertise and emotional support.

Brand positioning is the heartbeat of branding—it shapes how consumers perceive and remember your brand. When successfully executed, it differentiates your brand, connects with your target audience, and builds a robust brand image and reputation.

CHAPTER 8

THE ART OF BRAND EXPRESSION: MAKING YOUR BRAND SPEAK

In a crowded marketplace where countless brands compete for attention, how can you make your brand stand out? The answer lies in mastering the art of brand expression—the powerful means through which a brand communicates, visually, verbally, and experientially, with its target audience.

Brand expression encompasses a diverse array of elements that work in harmony to create a consistent and cohesive brand image. By leveraging these components, you can build brand recognition, awareness, and loyalty. Let's delve into the key ingredients that make up brand expression:

Brand Identity: The Visual Symphony

Think of brand identity as the visual symphony that represents your brand. It encompasses the tangible elements that form the face of your brand—the brand name, logo, tagline, color palette, typography, imagery, and other design elements. These visual elements come together to create a powerful visual identity that is consistently employed across all brand touchpoints. By establishing a visual connection, brand identity fosters brand recognition and leaves a lasting impression on your audience.

Consider a renowned healthcare organization known for its compassionate care. Its logo features a heart intertwined with hands, symbolizing the nurturing support and healing touch they provide. This visual representation resonates with patients, evoking a sense of trust and empathy even before any interaction takes place.

Brand Voice: The Harmonious Melody

Every brand possesses its own unique voice—an intangible quality that encompasses tone, style, and language. Brand voice is more than just the words you choose; it embodies the brand's personality, messaging, and tone of communication. Aligning your brand voice with your positioning, target audience, and overall brand strategy is paramount. A consistent and authentic brand voice establishes the brand's personality, builds connection, and reinforces a unified brand image across different communication channels.

Imagine a health supplement brand that embodies a holistic and empowering approach to wellness. Its brand voice is vibrant, empowering, and educational, using uplifting language and a friendly tone to engage its audience. Through consistent messaging, this brand builds trust, positioning itself as a knowledgeable ally on their wellness journey.

Brand Messaging: The Storyteller's Thread

Brand messaging weaves a powerful tapestry of key messages, value proposition, and brand story that resonates with your target audience. Clear, consistent, and aligned with your brand's positioning and values, brand messaging communicates your unique value proposition, benefits, and narrative. It serves as the storyteller's thread, shaping how your audience perceives and connects with your brand.

Consider a healthcare provider specializing in personalized patient care. Their brand messaging revolves around the story of a patient's transformative journey, highlighting individualized attention, compassionate support, and remarkable outcomes. By sharing these stories, the brand captivates their audience, evoking empathy and establishing itself as a beacon of hope.

Brand Experience: The Embrace of Connection

Brand experience is the tapestry of interactions and emotions that patients encounter at every touchpoint—whether in-store, online, during patient service, or through packaging and product/service usage. It is the lived expression of your brand, aligning with your brand's positioning, promise, and values. A positive and memorable brand experience leaves a lasting impression, fostering loyalty and advocacy among your patients.

Think of a dental clinic where patients are greeted with warm smiles, cozy waiting areas, and a soothing ambiance. Every aspect of the clinic's environment and patient service is meticulously designed to create a comforting and stress-free experience. This exceptional brand experience builds trust and loyalty, making patients feel valued and cared for.

Brand Assets: The Visual Storytellers

Brand assets serve as visual and verbal storytellers, conveying your brand's identity, messaging, and positioning through various marketing materials. These include advertisements, brochures, websites, social media content, packaging, signage, and other communication materials. By consistently reflecting your brand's identity, messaging, and positioning, brand assets create a unified and cohesive brand expression across different marketing channels.

Imagine a fitness brand whose social media posts exude energy, showcasing inspiring workout routines and sharing motivational stories of transformation. Their visual assets align with their brand's vibrant personality and position them as a go-to resource for fitness enthusiasts. With each post, they reinforce their brand expression, captivating and engaging their audience.

Brand Culture: The Essence Within

Brand culture encompasses the internal values, beliefs, and behaviors that permeate your organization. It shapes how your brand expression is manifested in all internal and external touchpoints. By fostering a positive and consistent brand culture, you reinforce your brand's expression, ensuring that it radiates through every employee and interaction.

Consider a healthcare organization whose employees embody empathy, professionalism, and a commitment to patient-centered care. These values are deeply embedded in their brand culture and are reflected in every interaction—from frontline staff to administrative personnel. This consistent brand culture ensures that the brand expression aligns with the promises made to patients, delivering a cohesive experience.

Brand expression is the gateway to building a strong and memorable brand image—one that resonates with your target audience. By thoughtfully and cohesively employing visual, verbal, and experiential elements, you can communicate your brand's identity, personality, messaging, and promise. Through a distinct and compelling brand expression, you'll leave an indelible mark in the minds of consumers.

CHAPTER 9

POWER OF BRAND CHARACTER:
UNLEASHING YOUR BRAND'S PERSONA

Imagine if your brand could come to life, possessing human-like qualities and forging emotional connections with your consumers. This is the magic of brand character—the ability to personify your brand, infusing it with unique characteristics and creating a relatable and memorable experience. In this chapter, we'll explore the transformative power of brand character and how it can propel your brand to new heights.

Brand character serves as the heartbeat of your brand strategy, influencing everything from messaging and tone of voice to visual elements and overall brand expression. It humanizes your brand, transcending mere functional attributes and touching the hearts of consumers. By forging an emotional connection, brand character paves the way for increased brand recognition, loyalty, and advocacy. Let's delve into the key aspects of brand character and its remarkable impact on your brand's success.

Breathing Life Into Your Brand: The Essence of Personality

Think of brand character as the essence of personality that defines your brand's identity. It encapsulates the human-like qualities, traits, and characteristics that consumers associate with your brand. By giving your brand a distinct personality, you create an emotional bond and foster familiarity with your target audience.

Consider a healthcare brand that embodies a friendly and approachable character. Through warm and inviting interactions, they create an atmosphere of trust and comfort for patients. From their website to social media posts, every touchpoint reflects their brand character, making patients feel like they're talking to a trusted friend rather than a faceless entity.

Crafting a Memorable Experience: The Art of Connection

Brand character plays a pivotal role in crafting a memorable experience for your consumers. By infusing your brand with specific traits and qualities, you create a unique and captivating encounter that resonates with your audience.

Imagine a skincare brand that embraces a fun-loving character. Through playful and humorous content, they inject joy and excitement into their consumers' daily routines. From colorful packaging to witty social media captions, every interaction leaves a smile on their customers' faces. This memorable experience deepens the emotional connection, making them advocates for the brand.

Aligning with Your Audience: Speaking Their Language

A well-defined brand character enables you to align with your target audience, speaking their language and forging a genuine connection. By understanding their values, aspirations, and preferences, you can tailor your brand character to resonate with their desires and beliefs.

Consider a luxury fashion brand that exudes sophistication and elegance. They understand their audience's desire for refinement and exclusivity. Through refined visuals, exquisite craftsmanship, and an aura of prestige, they appeal to consumers seeking a touch of luxury in their lives. This alignment establishes a deep connection and cultivates brand loyalty.

Consistency is Key: The Thread of Trust

Consistency in portraying your brand character is essential. By weaving a thread of trust, you ensure that every touchpoint conveys a cohesive and authentic brand experience.

Imagine a socially conscious brand that embodies a caring character. From sustainable packaging to philanthropic initiatives, every action reinforces their commitment to making a positive impact. Consistently demonstrating their caring character fosters trust among consumers, who appreciate the brand's genuine dedication to social responsibility.

Evolving and Adapting: The Dynamic Persona

While brand character provides a foundation, it is important to allow your brand's persona to evolve and adapt. Just as individuals grow and change, so too can your brand.

Consider an innovative tech brand that continuously pushes boundaries and embraces change. Their brand character evolves alongside technological advancements, staying ahead of the curve and remaining relevant to their tech-savvy audience. By embracing change and adaptability, they solidify their position as a visionary brand.

In conclusion, brand character breathes life into your brand, transforming it into a relatable and memorable persona. By defining and consistently expressing your brand's character traits, you create a powerful emotional connection with your audience. Through this connection, your brand becomes more than a mere entity—it becomes a trusted companion in the minds and hearts of consumers.

CHAPTER 10

THE ART OF VERBAL EXPRESSION: CRAFTING YOUR BRAND'S VOICE

In the vast world of branding, it's not just about how your brand looks—it's also about how it speaks. Verbal expression plays a vital role in shaping your brand's identity and forging connections with your audience. In this chapter, we'll explore the essential elements that make up a brand's verbal expression and the art of crafting a compelling brand voice.

Crafting Powerful Messages: The Magic of Brand Messaging

Brand messaging forms the foundation of your verbal expression. It encompasses the key messages and value proposition that you communicate to your target audience. Your brand's unique selling proposition (USP), brand promise, and story are all part of this crucial element. Effective brand messaging should be clear, concise, and aligned with your brand's positioning and values.

Let's take the example of a wellness brand that aims to inspire individuals to live healthier lives. Their brand messaging revolves around empowering their audience to make positive choices through their products and services. By communicating the brand's value, benefits, and differentiation, they inspire their customers to embrace a healthier lifestyle.

Setting the Right Tone: The Symphony of Words

Just like a composer sets the tone for a symphony, your brand must establish its own tone of voice. This refers to the attitude and style expressed in your brand's communication. It could be formal, informal, conversational, professional, friendly, authoritative, or any other tone that aligns with your brand's personality and target audience. Consistency in tone of voice across all touchpoints helps create a cohesive brand character.

Consider a fitness brand that exudes energy and motivation. Their tone of voice is vibrant, enthusiastic, and empowering. From their social media posts to customer interactions, every communication reflects their brand's dynamic and uplifting character. This consistency reinforces their brand image and fosters a deep connection with their audience.

The Language of Connection: Crafting the Right Style

Language style encompasses the choice of words, sentence structure, and grammar used in your brand's communication. It defines the style and manner in which your brand speaks to its audience. The language style you choose should be appropriate for your brand's target audience and consistently used across all communication channels.

Imagine a skincare brand that aims to provide a sense of luxury and indulgence. Their language style is elegant, sophisticated, and evocative. Through carefully crafted descriptions and captivating storytelling, they transport their audience into a world of beauty and self-care. This language style resonates with their customers, creating an aspirational experience.

The Power of a Name: Brand Name and Tagline

Your brand name and tagline are powerful verbal expressions that leave a lasting impression. The brand name should reflect your brand's identity, values, and positioning, while the tagline succinctly conveys your brand's value proposition or key messaging. Both the brand name and tagline should be memorable, meaningful, and aligned with your overall brand strategy.

Consider a healthcare brand with a mission to provide compassionate and patient-centered care. Their brand name evokes a sense of trust and empathy, while their tagline captures their commitment to putting patients first. This combination of a meaningful brand name and a resonant tagline creates a strong foundation for their verbal expression.

Captivating with Words: Content and Copywriting

Content and copywriting form the backbone of your brand's communication. Whether it's website content, social media posts, advertising copy, or other written materials, they play a pivotal role in conveying your brand's messaging, tone of voice, and language style. Effective content and copywriting should effectively communicate your brand's value, benefits, and story.

Imagine a nutrition brand that aims to educate and inspire its audience to embrace healthier eating habits. Through informative blog posts, engaging social media content, and persuasive product descriptions, they empower their customers to make informed choices. Their content and copywriting consistently reflect their brand's messaging and create a compelling narrative.

Unleashing the Power of Stories: Brand Storytelling

One of the most potent forms of verbal expression is brand storytelling. It involves weaving together your brand's story, history, values, and purpose in a compelling and engaging way. Brand storytelling helps create an emotional connection with consumers and builds a memorable brand image. This can be done through various content formats, such as videos, blogs, social media posts, and other brand communication materials.

Let's take the example of a wellness brand that shares the personal journeys of individuals who have transformed their lives through healthier choices. By showcasing these inspiring stories through video testimonials and blog articles, they create an emotional bond with their audience. This storytelling approach resonates deeply with customers, as they can relate to real-life experiences.

The verbal expression of your brand is a powerful tool for building a strong and coherent brand voice. By carefully crafting your brand messaging, establishing the right tone of voice, choosing the appropriate language style, creating a memorable brand name and tagline, leveraging effective content and copywriting, and harnessing the power of brand storytelling, you can create a verbal expression that resonates with your audience and leaves a lasting impact.

In the next chapter, we delve into the captivating world of visual expression and explore how to create a visually compelling brand identity. Join us as we uncover the secrets to designing a captivating visual presence that reflects the essence of your brand.

CHAPTER 11

THE ART OF VISUAL EXPRESSION: CREATING A LASTING IMPRESSION

When it comes to branding, visual expression is like a language that speaks directly to the eyes and emotions of your audience. It encompasses the visual elements and design choices that represent and communicate your brand's identity, personality, and values. In this chapter, we explore the captivating world of visual expression and how it plays a pivotal role in creating a distinct and memorable brand image.

The Emblem of Identity: The Power of a Logo

At the heart of visual expression lies your brand's logo—the iconic symbol that serves as a visual representation of your brand's identity. A well-crafted logo combines symbols, icons, typography, and colors to convey your brand's personality, values, and positioning. It becomes the face of your brand, gracing packaging, signage, websites, social media platforms, and various marketing materials, ensuring consistent brand recognition.

Think of the world's most recognized logos, such as the golden arches of McDonald's or the swoosh of Nike. These logos have become synonymous with their respective brands, instantly evoking recognition and familiarity. A meticulously designed logo has the power to leave a lasting impression in the minds of consumers.

The Language of Colors: Creating Emotional Connections

Colors possess an extraordinary ability to evoke emotions and convey meanings. A brand's color palette is thoughtfully chosen to align with its personality, positioning, and target audience. It consists of primary colors, secondary colors, and accent colors that are consistently used across various brand materials to create a cohesive visual identity.

For example, the vibrant red of Coca-Cola signifies energy and passion, while the serene blue of Facebook exudes trust and reliability. Each color has a purpose and plays a role in shaping the overall brand experience. When applied consistently, colors become an integral part of your brand's visual expression, triggering emotions and forging connections with your audience.

The Art of Typography: Conveying Tone and Style

Typography is the art of selecting and arranging fonts and typefaces to visually communicate your brand's message. The choice of typography significantly impacts your brand's visual expression, conveying its personality, tone, and style. Brands often establish typography guidelines that define the fonts to be used in different brand materials, including headings, body text, and other design elements.

Consider the elegant script of a high-end fashion brand or the bold and modern typefaces of a tech startup. The typography choices not only complement the brand's visual elements but also communicate the brand's character and style. Consistency in typography ensures that your brand's voice is heard loud and clear across all touchpoints.

Visual Storytelling: The Power of Imagery

Imagery breathes life into your brand's visual expression. It encompasses photography, illustrations, graphics, and other visual elements that reinforce your brand's identity. The style and type of imagery used should align with your brand's personality, values, and target audience. Whether it's the striking visuals of a travel brand or the heartwarming images of a charitable organization, the right imagery can evoke emotions, convey narratives, and build connections with your audience.

Imagine a sports apparel brand using powerful action shots of athletes to ignite a sense of inspiration and determination in their audience. By carefully curating imagery that aligns with their brand's visual identity, they create a visual story that resonates with their customers, motivating them to push their limits.

The Blueprint of Consistency: Visual Guidelines

To ensure consistency in your brand's visual expression, it's essential to develop visual guidelines or a style guide. These guidelines provide instructions on how to use visual elements such as logos, colors, typography, and imagery in different brand materials, maintaining a cohesive and unified visual identity. They serve as a blueprint for designers, ensuring that your brand's visual expression remains consistent across various touchpoints.

Visual guidelines empower your team and external partners to create cohesive brand experiences. They establish boundaries while encouraging creativity, allowing your brand to shine through in every visual interaction.

Crafting the Visual Symphony: The Design Style

The design style is the conductor of your brand's visual expression, harmonizing the layout, composition, and overall aesthetics of your visual elements. It should align with your brand's personality, target audience, and positioning, creating a visually appealing and engaging brand image.

Think about a luxury fashion brand that meticulously designs its visuals with sleek and sophisticated aesthetics, exuding an air of exclusivity and refinement. By carefully crafting the design style, they create an immersive experience that captivates their audience and reinforces their brand's identity.

The visual expression of your brand holds immense power in creating a lasting impression. By strategically designing your logo, harnessing the language of colors, mastering typography, curating impactful imagery, establishing visual guidelines, and crafting a harmonious design style, you can create a visual identity that resonates with your audience and leaves an indelible mark.

CHAPTER 12

REPUTATION MANAGEMENT: BUILDING TRUST AND SHAPING PERCEPTIONS

In the realm of branding, reputation management takes center stage as a crucial practice that guides how a brand is perceived by the public. It involves a strategic approach to monitoring, shaping, and maintaining the overall perception of a brand among its target audience, stakeholders, and the general public. In this chapter, we delve into the intricate world of reputation management and its profound impact on a brand's success.

The Essence of Reputation: A Valuable Asset

A brand's reputation is an intangible asset that embodies the perceptions, opinions, and attitudes people hold towards the brand. It is a reflection of the interactions and experiences individuals have had with the brand, including product quality, customer service, brand messaging, social responsibility, and more. A positive brand reputation fosters increased trust, loyalty, and advocacy, while a negative reputation can lead to a loss of patients, sales, and overall brand value.

Imagine a healthcare provider with a stellar reputation for compassionate care, cutting-edge treatments, and exceptional patient experiences. The positive reputation they have cultivated over the years inspires confidence and attracts new patients, setting them apart from their competitors. On the other hand, a healthcare provider with a tarnished reputation may struggle to regain patient trust and loyalty.

Listening and Shaping: The Power of Perception

Reputation management begins with actively monitoring and listening to what people are saying about the brand across various channels, both online and offline. This includes social media platforms, review sites, news outlets, and patient feedback. By paying attention to these channels, brands can identify potential reputation issues early on and take appropriate actions to address them.

Crafting a strong brand messaging and communication strategy is also pivotal in shaping a brand's reputation. Consistency is key, as messaging should align with the brand's values, positioning, and target audience. Clear, authentic, and transparent communication fosters trust and contributes to building and maintaining a positive reputation.

Patient Experience: The Heart of Reputation

Providing exceptional patient experiences and ensuring patient satisfaction is at the core of reputation management. Every touchpoint with a patient contributes to their perception of the brand. By delivering outstanding care, attentive service, and personalized interactions, brands can leave a lasting positive impression on their patients. Satisfied patients become brand advocates, sharing their positive experiences and contributing to a strong reputation.

Consider a dental practice that goes the extra mile to create a comfortable and welcoming environment for their patients. From the moment patients step into the clinic to the care they receive during their appointments, every interaction is designed to exceed expectations. This commitment to exceptional patient experience not only builds patient loyalty but also enhances the practice's reputation within the community.

Navigating Challenges: Crisis Management

Brands must be prepared to handle potential crises or negative situations that may arise. Developing a comprehensive crisis management plan is essential for effective reputation management. It involves promptly addressing any issues, providing transparent communication, and taking appropriate actions to mitigate any negative impact on the brand's reputation.

In times of crisis, open and honest communication becomes paramount. By acknowledging mistakes, demonstrating accountability, and outlining steps taken to rectify the situation, brands can rebuild trust and salvage their reputation. The ability to navigate challenges with grace and transparency can significantly influence how a brand is perceived in the face of adversity.

Cultivating Brand Advocacy: The Power of Engagement

To proactively shape their reputation, brands can engage with patients, stakeholders, and influencers to build brand advocacy. Leveraging social media platforms, participating in community initiatives, partnering with influencers, and encouraging positive user-generated content can all contribute to enhancing a brand's reputation.

Imagine a wellness brand that actively engages with its online community by sharing informative content, responding to comments, and fostering meaningful conversations. By nurturing a sense of belonging and actively listening to their audience's needs, they create a community of brand advocates who champion their products and services, thus bolstering their reputation.

The Digital Landscape: Online Reputation Management

In today's digital era, managing a brand's online reputation is crucial. This involves monitoring and responding to online reviews, comments, and mentions, addressing any negative content, and promoting positive content to influence the online perception of the brand. By actively managing their online presence, brands can shape their digital reputation and reinforce their desired image.

Reputation management is an ongoing journey that requires consistent effort, vigilance, and strategic actions. Cultivating a positive reputation contributes to a strong brand image, patient trust, and long-term success. By listening and shaping perceptions, prioritizing exceptional patient experiences, navigating challenges with resilience, fostering brand advocacy, and managing their digital presence, brands can build and maintain a reputation that resonates with their audience and sets them apart from the competition.

In a later chapter, we explore the realm of brand storytelling and how it can captivate hearts and minds, forging deeper connections with patients and creating a lasting impact. Join us as we uncover the art of crafting compelling narratives that bring brands to life.

Chapter 13

DEFINING YOUR BRAND

The golden arches of McDonald's and the Nike swoosh did not become what they are in a day. These and other successful brands are the product of careful research, distinctly defined boundaries and a comprehensive Marketing strategy. The result of all this hard work is that each patient and potential patient knows exactly what these brands represent.

Have you ever walked into McDonald's to order to purchase a Pepperoni pizza? Will anyone in their right minds drive to Nike to pick up a pair of ruby red stilettos?

Of course not! That is as a result of these brands being so carefully defined that we know exactly what to expect and what these brands can deliver.

Customers are far more likely to be loyal to a brand that sends a clear message or has a distinct voice.

The first step to defining your brand is developing the **Brand Strategy**. This involves defining the brand's purpose, vision, mission, and values. It includes understanding the target audience, competitive landscape, and market positioning.

As Simon Sinek states in his book of the same name, when brands "start with why" they start with their purpose. So, let's get down to it.

For the next few sections, you may want to pull out a notebook and actually answer the questions as we go through them. By doing so, you will develop a background & foundational document for your practice upon which your branding and marketing strategies can be built.

Purpose

What does your business do? I know you're a service provider, and in the healthcare field, or you've picked up the wrong book - lol. What I need to know is what services you offer. Why do you provide those services? And NO, the answer is NOT to make money! Dig deeper. What changes are you trying to affect?

For Example: With my business Neurotic Dog Studios, I provide branding and graphic services. But that's not the whole story. I want to help other businesses change the world. Branding & graphics are not going to be a change-maker in and of itself, but I can help businesses to get recognized for the benefits they provide to their community, help them appear professional, and attract the investors that they need to make change happen. I see that the best ideas and businesses can still fail due to bad branding and reputation management, and I don't want to see companies that have a mission to better the world fail before they have a chance to get started. So, my services may be design in nature but my purpose is to change the world, one person, one community, and one project at a time.

So, what is it that you do? And why do you do it? Why are you in business? What are you so passionate about that you were forced to do this and not something else? Who are you as people? What business or category do you compete in? Why does it matter? (This is controlled by the patient... so think from THEIR perspective. Why should they care you are there?)

Once you understand your purpose it will be easier for you to develop your mission statement, vision & your values. The purpose of your business should never change.

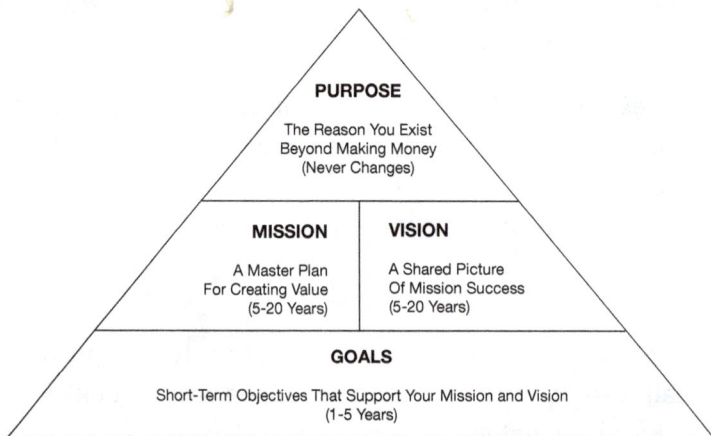

PURPOSE
The Reason You Exist
Beyond Making Money
(Never Changes)

MISSION
A Master Plan
For Creating Value
(5-20 Years)

VISION
A Shared Picture
Of Mission Success
(5-20 Years)

GOALS
Short-Term Objectives That Support Your Mission and Vision
(1-5 Years)

Vision

The vision is the aspirations of the brand and the ambition of how the leadership envisions the brand in the future. Your vision is a shared picture of mission success. It's the view of what achieving your mission would look like over the next 5 to 20 years. It offers guidance to where the brand is going and puts markers in the ground for what the brand aims to achieve.

> **Exercise:** Take 20 minutes and write an obituary for your business. Imagine your company is "dead" 25 years from now. You are in charge of writing the obituary. What did the business accomplish? How was it viewed by its patients? What great things did the company do? Did it change the world? Did it leave the world a better place? What impact did it make? Go big. You have NO limitations. This is your opportunity to envision just what you want the business to be.

Once you have that written out now the question is "What do you need to do to make it a reality?"

Mission

Let's look at your mission. The brand mission represents what the brand is committed to in order to arrive at that vision of the future brand. These commitments are related to the day-to-day operations of the brand and are made to the audience it serves. It is typically based on the 5-to-20-year plan. Your mission is the action steps you are going to take to get to your vision.

Your vision and mission are supported by the many small, short-term goals.

Values

The brand values represent how the brand will behave in the marketplace and what it holds dear in its dealings. Many brands claim to have core values, but few hold them dear as a philosophy for how they do business. You need to think of your values as the compass for your company. They guide and direct your business and your people this is why it is so important that you REMEMBER that you MUST be authentic in your values.

Don't say that you value people, and then treat your employees like cogs in a machine. Or, say you are environmentally conscious and then back endeavors that cut down the rain forest or pollute the oceans. You need to seriously consider what you want your business's values to be and then how are you going to ensure that those values are maintained. Culture matters.

The **least paid and lowest status employee** is often the first contact that your potential patient has with your business. Do they have a reason to exhibit the values that you want your company to have? Do these values permeate each level of your organization? As your business grows (and eventually silos) this becomes a more challenging commitment.

Start your business as you want it to go and make sure that you have full buy-in between management and staff at each level or you will suffer from inauthenticity – and this *will* undermine your brand.

CHAPTER 14

OUR EMPLOYEES: DO THEY UNDERSTAND OUR BRAND?

Many companies don't stop to think about how their employees see the organization when looking at the company branding. However, it's crucial to understand your employees' feelings about the company. By understanding how your company is perceived and its internal culture, you can develop strategies that will enable you to manage and guide the companies brand from the inside.

Let's take a moment to examine a company's internal interactions. Do your employees know & understand the organization's values? Are they felt "lived" within the company? Are they shown at each step of the management / subordinate process? Are there any processes in place that hold leaders accountable in how they treat their subordinates?

Is the organization one cohesive unit, or has it grown to the point where silos have developed? Once an organization has started to split off into departmental silos, it becomes more challenging to maintain a cohesive culture. So, it's essential to examine and address cultural issues early and often.

How are inter-organizational communications handled? Are employees aware of the overarching mission and goals of the company? It may be easier to keep information confined to the management and on a need-to-know basis. Still, if you don't have open communication — as much as strategically possible, anyhow — you will end up creating a culture of secrecy, and secrecy can build distrust. If your employees are not engaged, they don't have any incentive to reflect the company values to others in the organization or to clients and patients.

When you are focusing on internal culture. You need to be looking at how it would be supported, evaluated, and applied. There are six components of company culture: three about creating a vision and three about bringing that cultural vision to life.

The first components should be familiar after the previous chapters: Purpose (the organization's purpose – beyond making money); Values (shared belief about WHAT is most important when conducting business), and; Behaviors (employee made choices that are guided by the purpose & values).

The last three components bring these to life: Recognition programs that encourage behaviors that support the desired culture. Rituals – group activities that build and strengthen relationships, Cues – reminders that help employees and leaders to stay connected to the future.

For a comprehensive examination into developing a company's internal culture, I recommend exploring *Great Mondays* by Josh Levine. He delves into the six components of culture. He then looks beyond into the development of external community culture and how to keep a company afloat on the constantly changing tides of community and purpose.

CHAPTER 15

WHO ARE OUR COMPETITORS?

To better understand where your business stands within your community and ecosystem, first, you need to identify the parameters of that context.

Defining the context for your business includes:
- looking at the geography that your business encompasses
- the project/companies/etc. that are competing for your patient's attention
- spending thresholds
- look for other limiting factors that would narrow the field
- determine your prominent competitors

If you understand who your patients are and what their focus is, you start to eliminate concerns about competitors because you will find that they do not aligned with your patient base.

Now that you've identified your competitors rank them from one to three, one as the most direct competitor. If you identify more than three, you can continue the process by just going through the same questions listed for them.

For each of the competitor you have identified:

1. List out the characteristics that make them a competitor for your practice.

      a. Do they service the same market? _____

      b. Are they offering the same products/services? _____

      _____

      _____

      c. Do they provide similar quality? _____

      _____

      _____

Break down each element that contributes to their status as competition.

2. Where are they within the market strata?

    a. Are they the leader of the field? _____

    b. Or is their market share non-existent? _____

Knowing where they rank can help you identify which competitors you need to focus on to move up the standings in recognition and prominence.

3. What is the market position for each of your competitors?

    a. Are they focused exclusively on a particular nitch? _____

    _____

    b. Is there pricing the essential factor impacting patient decision-making? _____

    _____

    c. What about quality, convenience, patient service? _____

    _____

    _____

    d. What elements differentiate them from other competitors within the consumer's mind?_____

    _____

    _____

    _____

4. What do your competitors promise to their patients? Is it excellent patient service? Your happiness or your money back? The brand promise should be something easily identified. _____

_____

_____

5. Describe your competition as a person. Remember, I told you that one of the best ways to work through branding is by imagining your business as a person. The same is true with your competitor's branding. Describe your competitor's color, attitude, music. Are they aggressive, helpful, caring, indifferent?

_____

_____

_____

_____

_____

_____

_____

_____

_____

6. In looking at your competitor's strengths, what things do they do well. Where are they in the field? At what does your competitor excel? What are the socially-know positives? _____

_____

_____

_____

_____

7. Just as we examine their strengths, we need to look at their weaknesses. What does your competitor do poorly? Where do they receive the majority of their criticism? What are the socially-know negatives? _____

_____

_____

_____

_____

Your Differentiation

Now that you understand more about your competition, how do you differ from them? _____

_____

_____

_____

_____

What makes your business unique? _____

_____

_____

_____

_____

Do you focus on a different audience or niche? _____

_____

_____

Are your services/products superior quality? _____

_____

_____

_____

Your brand positioning statement.

Our [**offering**] is the only [**category**] that [**benefit**].

Example: Our [**branding workbook**] is the only [**free resource**] that [**guides you through each step of identifying your current brand with explanatory email lessons**].

Your turn:

Our _____ is the only _____
_____ that _____.

Or use a comprehensive format:

[**Company Name**] is the only [**category**] that [**differentiation characteristic**] for [**patient**] in [**market geography**] who [**need state**] during [**underlying trend**].

Example: [**Neurotic Dog Studios**] is the only [**Branding & Design Agency**] that [**is passionate about the plight of special-need & disabled individuals**] for [**businesses wanting to improve their communities**] in [**the United States**] who [**need branding and a professional appearance to obtain funding, recognition, and clients**].

_____ is the only _____ that _____
_____ for _____
in _____ who _____ during
_____.

CHAPTER 16

UNDERSTANDING YOUR PATIENTS: UNCOVERING INSIGHTS FOR EFFECTIVE BRANDING

In today's competitive healthcare landscape, building a successful brand requires a deep understanding of your patients. By conducting thorough research and gathering insights from your target audience, you can create a brand that resonates with their needs, desires, and emotions. This chapter delves into the importance of patient research, asking the right questions, and developing buyer personas to guide your branding strategies effectively.

Conducting a Brand Audit

To gauge how your patients perceive your brand, conducting a brand audit is crucial. This process involves evaluating their current opinions, beliefs, and experiences related to your brand and its offerings. By collecting data and feedback, you can gain valuable insights into their perspectives and identify any misconceptions or misunderstandings.

A brand audit also provides an opportunity to assess how your brand fares against competitors. Understanding how patients perceive your brand in relation to others helps you identify your unique selling points and areas for improvement. By conducting online surveys, in-house questionnaires, or engaging in direct conversations, you can gather a wealth of information to inform your branding decisions.

Asking the Right Questions

Effective research relies on asking the right questions. By framing clear, concise, and direct inquiries, you can extract valuable insights from your patients. Consider the words of Thomas Berger, who noted that the art and science of asking questions are the source of all knowledge. When designing surveys or questionnaires, ensure that the questions are straightforward and get straight to the point.

However, it's equally important to be cautious of asking wrong or misleading questions, as Ursula K. Le Guin pointed out that there are no right answers to wrong questions. To extract meaningful responses, focus on questions that explore patients' perceptions, expectations, and experiences. By gathering data through well-designed surveys and questionnaires, you can gain valuable insights that inform your branding efforts.

Understanding the Emotional Connection

Branding is not solely about numbers and statistics; it's about emotions and differentiation. To truly connect with your patients, it's important to understand the emotional factors that drive their decisions. Take a step back and reflect on why patients choose your practice or healthcare services. What do they truly want, and how does your offering make a positive impact on their lives?

Delve deeper into the emotional underpinnings behind their decisions to connect with your practice. Identify the emotional benefits and motivations that drive their choices. Does your brand offer a sense of prestige or exclusivity? Does it provide a solution to their pain or discomfort? Understanding these emotional connections allows you to develop a stronger bond with your patients and tailor your branding efforts to resonate with their desires and aspirations.

Developing Buyer Personas

Buyer personas are generalized representations of your ideal patients. These personas capture the common characteristics, preferences, and needs of specific patient segments. Developing detailed buyer personas helps humanize your target audience and guides your branding strategies by aligning them with your patients' motivations and behaviors.

Start by collecting basic demographic information, such as age, gender, occupation, and location. This provides a foundation for understanding the composition of your patient base. However, a comprehensive buyer persona goes beyond demographics. It dives deeper into psychographic factors, including their values, interests, lifestyle, and aspirations.

To develop accurate buyer personas, leverage the insights you gather from patient research and interactions. Look for patterns and commonalities in their feedback, preferences, and motivations. By understanding your patients' shared characteristics, you can create targeted marketing campaigns, craft personalized messaging, and develop products or services that truly meet their needs.

Reaching Your Target Audience

Once you have a clear understanding of your target audience, it is crucial to develop a strategy that effectively engages and connects with them. However, it is important to strike a balance between promoting your brand and respecting your audience's boundaries. Instead of constantly selling your products or services, aim to capture their interest, initiate conversations, and foster genuine engagement.

Here are some strategies to captivate your target audience:

1. Thought-provoking questions: Start discussions around current events or relevant topics that encourage your audience to share their perspectives. This approach stimulates interaction and encourages active participation.

2. How-to videos: Create instructional videos related to hobbies or activities that align with your buyer personas. Provide useful information that helps your audience while fostering a sense of connection and expertise.

3. Exciting giveaways: Organize contests or promotions that encourage your audience to share pictures or stories related to your products or services. This generates excitement and user-generated content, fostering a sense of involvement and anticipation.

4. Humorous memes: Share memes or humorous content that resonates with your target audience's sense of humor. This lighthearted approach helps create a relatable and enjoyable

connection.

5. Curated content: Share valuable content from other brands or sources that your audience would find useful. By positioning your brand as a trusted resource, you build credibility and reinforce your relevance in your audience's lives.

6. Participating in trending challenges: Engage in popular challenges or trends that align with your brand values. This fosters a sense of community and shared experiences, allowing you to connect with your audience on a deeper level.

Expanding on reaching your target audience:

1. Social Media Marketing: Utilize various social media platforms to connect with your target audience. Develop a comprehensive strategy that includes creating engaging content, sharing industry news, running targeted ad campaigns, and actively interacting with your followers.

2. Influencer Marketing: Collaborate with influencers or thought leaders who have a strong following and credibility among your target audience. Partnering with influencers can help you expand your reach and build trust through authentic endorsements and recommendations.

3. Content Marketing: Create valuable and informative content that addresses the pain points, challenges, and interests of your target audience. Develop a content strategy that includes blog posts, articles, videos, podcasts, infographics, and downloadable resources. Optimize your content for search engines to improve visibility and attract organic traffic.

4. Email Marketing: Build an email list by offering valuable content, exclusive promotions, or newsletters to your website visitors or customers. Use targeted and personalized messages to deliver relevant content and nurture leads. Segment your email list based on demographics, interests, or engagement levels.

5. Search Engine Optimization (SEO): Optimize your website and online content to rank higher in search engine results. Conduct keyword research and create content that aligns with your audience's needs. Improve technical aspects, page load speed, and build quality backlinks to enhance search engine visibility.

6. Paid Advertising: Utilize online advertising platforms to reach your target audience directly. Set up targeted ad campaigns based on demographics, interests, or online behaviors. Monitor and optimize your campaigns to maximize effectiveness and ROI.

7. Community Engagement: Participate in online forums, social media groups, or industry-specific communities where your target audience is active. Provide valuable insights, answer questions, and engage in meaningful discussions to establish yourself as a trusted authority.

8. Offline Marketing: Don't overlook the power of offline marketing strategies. Consider traditional advertising methods such as print ads, billboards, direct mail, or hosting local events. Sponsor relevant community events or participate in industry conferences and trade shows to connect with your audience in person.

9. Referral Programs: Encourage satisfied customers to refer your products or services to others. Implement a referral program that rewards both the referrer and the referred, incentivizing word-of-mouth marketing and expanding your reach through trusted recommendations.

10. Collaborations and Partnerships: Seek opportunities to collaborate with complementary businesses or organizations that share your target audience. Co-host webinars or events, cross-promote each other's content, or bundle products or services together. Collaborations can help you tap into a new audience and benefit from the credibility and reach of your partners.

Remember, to reach your target audience effectively, it is crucial to understand their preferences, behaviors, and communication channels. Continuously monitor and analyze your marketing efforts to optimize your strategies and adapt to evolving trends and preferences.

Understanding User Intent for SEO

Understanding user intent is crucial when implementing search engine optimization (SEO) techniques to attract new patients. Instead of solely focusing on keywords, it is important to consider the underlying purpose behind users' search queries. Generally, users have three main intentions when conducting online searches: finding a location, understanding a topic, or learning how to do something.

By aligning your keyword strategy with these intentions, you can create content that directly addresses the specific needs of patients and provides them with relevant information. This approach enhances the overall user experience and increases the likelihood of your content being shared, benefiting both your audience and your brand.

1. Finding a location: Many users search online to find a specific location, such as a medical practice or healthcare facility near them. To cater to this user intent, optimize your content by including relevant location-based keywords. This can include specifying the areas you serve, mentioning nearby landmarks, or providing directions and contact information. By incorporating these location-specific elements, you make it easier for potential patients to find and connect with your practice.

2. Understanding a topic: Users often turn to search engines to gain a better understanding of a particular topic or medical condition. To address this user intent, create informative and educational content that covers various aspects of the topic at hand. Conduct thorough research to identify common questions or concerns related to the topic and provide detailed answers. Utilize relevant keywords that align with the users' search

queries, ensuring that your content is easily discoverable and meets their informational needs.

3. Learning how to do something: Another common user intent is to seek instructions or guidance on how to perform a specific task or procedure. To cater to this intent, develop content that provides step-by-step instructions, tutorials, or informative guides. Incorporate relevant keywords that reflect the specific task or procedure, making it easier for users to find the information they need. You can also utilize different content formats such as videos or infographics to enhance the instructional value and engagement of your content.

By understanding and aligning your keyword strategy with these user intentions, you can create targeted content that directly addresses patients' needs. This not only enhances their experience by providing them with valuable and relevant information but also increases the likelihood of your content being shared and recommended to others. As a result, your brand gains visibility, credibility, and trust among your target audience.

Continuously analyze and monitor user search behavior, keyword trends, and search engine algorithms to refine your SEO strategy. By staying updated with the evolving user intent and search landscape, you can adapt your content and optimization techniques to effectively meet the needs of your target audience and maintain a competitive edge in the digital healthcare landscape.

Sharing Relevant Content from Other Brands

While building your own brand, don't hesitate to share content from other brands that align with your audience's interests and needs. Sharing relevant and valuable content demonstrates that your primary goal is to provide value and assist your patients, rather than purely promoting your own products or services.

However, exercise caution when sharing content from competing brands within your niche. Such actions may be misinterpreted as a direct attack or an attempt to surrender. Instead, focus on sharing news reports, inspirational quotes, or instructional videos that your audience will find beneficial and appreciate.

Emphasizing Consistency and Effective Messaging

To maintain a consistent brand message, it's essential to avoid repetitive content across multiple platforms. Posting identical images, videos, and information on various channels can make your brand appear lazy or overly pushy. Instead, adopt a focused approach that aligns with the objectives of your company.

For example, if your product or service aims to improve patients' health, you can directly sell its benefits. Alternatively, you can promote a holistic approach by sharing content from other sources that features easy workout videos and healthy meal preparation guides. By subtly emphasizing the benefits of your offerings, you can maintain a consistent message while avoiding repetitive content.

Understanding your patients is the cornerstone of effective branding. By conducting research, asking the right questions, and developing buyer personas, you gain valuable insights into your target audience's preferences, motivations, and aspirations. With this knowledge, you can create relevant and engaging content, establish a strong emotional connection, and build a successful brand that resonates with your patients.

PART 3

CREATING YOUR BRAND

"A brand is not just a logo or a product, it's an experience." -

— Seth Godin,
marketing author & speaker

Seth Godin is a renowned marketing author and speaker recognized for his unconventional and innovative approach to marketing and entrepreneurship. With over 20 books to his name, such as "Purple Cow" and "Permission Marketing," Godin challenges traditional marketing norms and encourages businesses to create remarkable products, build meaningful relationships with customers, and embrace change in the digital age. His thought-provoking writings have had a significant impact on the industry, inspiring marketers and entrepreneurs to think differently and make a lasting impact through their marketing efforts.

In addition to his writing, Seth Godin is a highly sought-after speaker known for his engaging presentations. His work has made him an influential figure in the marketing world, challenging conventional wisdom and providing valuable insights that have inspired a new era of marketing strategies.

CHAPTER 17

SCULPTING AN IDENTITY

Now that you have embarked on the journey of self-discovery and gained a deeper understanding of who you are as an practice, it is time to translate that knowledge into shaping your desired identity.

This section of the book is not for you to passively read. I fully expect your interaction. If will do you no good to read these pages and do nothing, so I am creating space — here, IN THIS BOOK, for you to write your answer. If you just can not bring yourself to write in a book (or you have a audio/digital version), you can visit brandingyourpractice. com/downloads.

Practice Name: A Reflection of Your Essence

Take a moment to reflect on your practice's name. Does it still embody the essence of who you are?

_____

_____

Consider whether any changes within the practice warrant a name change. Moreover, assess the perception of your name within the community. Does it hold a positive standing?

_____

_____

Conversely, have there been any negative events associated with your practice that could be mitigated through a name change?

_____

_____

Caution must be exercised here since merely changing a name to minimize bad press, without any philosophical changes, can backfire.

However, if approached with a genuine shift in values, a name change can be a positive move. Transparency plays a crucial role in such transitions, helping stakeholders understand the reasoning behind the change.

Logo and Colors: Visual Representation of Your Essence

Your practice's logo serves as the initial introduction to the world. Consider whether it conveys the message you want to send about your practice.

Does it align with your history and the evolution of your practice?

_____

_____

_____

Moreover, assess whether the colors employed in your logo are appropriate for your industry and resonate with your patients. Do they help you stand out from your competitors?

_____

_____

Evaluating the recognition and reception of your logo by your patient base is crucial in determining its effectiveness.

It may intrigue you why we begin our exploration with the name and logo of your practice. The reason is simple but significant. Evaluating whether you require a facelift or a complete overhaul allows you to consider the option of rebranding. Rebranding entails a comprehensive transformation that necessitates professional assistance in developing both a new name convention and logo. However, please note that if you opt for rebranding, it does not mean you should stop here. All the work you have done and will continue to do plays a vital role in guiding your designers, marketing strategists, and any other professionals involved, helping them understand your journey from where you were to where you aspire to be.

SWOT Chart: Evaluating Your Strengths, Weaknesses, Opportunities, and Threats

Enter your Strengths, Weaknesses, Opportunities, and Threats (SWOT) into the chart below. Incorporate any additional insights gained throughout this book. The SWOT analysis acts as a valuable tool in understanding your practice's internal strengths and weaknesses, as well as external opportunities and threats.

SWOT MATRIX	STRENGTHS	WEAKNESSES
Strengths & Weaknesses are "Internal" Opportunities and Threats are "External" Create strategies for the intersection of the S & W with the O & T		
OPPORTUNITIES	S/O STRATEGIES	W/O STRATEGIES
THREATS	S/T STRATEGIES	W/T STRATEGIES

If you need prompts for the SWOT chart...

Strengths:
- What do we do well?
- What about our practice do we feel proud of?
- What traits or abilities does our practice have that will help us to reach future success?
- What do our patients and staff say about us?

Weaknesses:
- What aspects of our practice do we need to work on?
- What makes our practice vulnerable to threats?
- What traits or abilities of the practice are weak?
- What frustrations or disappointments do we or our patients encounter with the practice?

Opportunities:
- What trends or events are creating more opportunities locally or globally?
- What changes in technology can we take advantage of?
- What government policies are in effect that could have significant positive influence on our practice?
- What cultural or social changes are creating opportunities for our practice?

Threats:
- What obstacle(s) are we facing in the environment? (economics, trends, government regulations, labor market, conditions, etc.)
- What market trends affect us (e.g., demand, competition, industry changes)?
- Is changing technology a threat?

Goals, Mission Statement, Values: Defining Your Direction

First, let's take a moment and write down your practices established goals, missing statement & values. If you need a refresher, refer back to Chapter 13: Defining Your Brand where we talked about your practice and what your purpose, vision, mission and values are.

Goals: _____

_____

_____

_____

_____

_____

Assess whether your goals accurately reflect your desired trajectory. If not, this is the opportune moment to re-evaluate and develop new Organizational goals.

Mission Statement: _____

_____

_____

_____

_____

Next, scrutinize your practice's mission statement. Considering the exploration you have undertaken to understand who your practice truly is, reflect on whether your mission statement still aligns with your essence. If not, seize this opportunity to develop a new mission statement that accurately represents your purpose.

Values: _____

_____

_____

_____

_____

_____

Values hold immense significance in defining your practice's identity. Examine both the "officially" stated values and the values that have genuinely been "lived" within your practice. Once again, this is the ideal time to make any necessary changes.

Ensure that the goals, mission statement, and values resonate with what you express your practice cares. Does it support your practices purpose?

Now, take a step back and assess whether your practice can effectively support your goals, mission statement, and values in light of the insights gained from the SWOT analysis from earlier in this chapter. If you identify any challenges, note them down, as they will inform your strategic decision-making.

_____

_____

_____

_____

_____

Patients/Target Audience: Cultivating Meaningful Connections

Were going to start with defining our base patient. Their demographics and psychographics. For this exercise I want you to select one patient who represents the type of patient you would like to have more of. With this person in mind, answer the following...

How old are they?_____

Race?_____

Gender?_____

Income level?_____

Where do they live?_____

Are they married?_____

Do they have children?_____

Are they who we want as patients?_____

Why?_____

_____

_____

What do our patients think about us?_____

Do they know what we stand for?_____

Do they know our mission statement?_____

Are their interactions with our practice in line with who we think we are?_____

_____

What do they tell their friends and family about us?_____

_____

_____

Why, if they are repeat patients, do they continue to use us?_____

_____

_____

Can they recognize us (our services, products, materials) from our competitors?_____

_____

_____

What do our patients come to us initially?_____

_____

_____

Does this representation accurately capture the patient base your practice aspires to have? Revise and refine the information as necessary to complete the persona worksheet below. Understanding your target audience is paramount in crafting tailored strategies and engaging with your patients in meaningful ways.

Patient Experience: Designing the Ideal Encounter

Envision the ideal experience for your patients. Describe it in vivid detail, utilizing all five senses to bring it to life. Consider the following questions as a starting point:

How are patients greeted?_____

_____

_____

Is it... ☐ in person   ☐ on the phone   ☐ an automated system

Does the patient already know who your practice is and what it does? Yes / No, If yes, how did they become aware of you?

_____

_____

_____

_____

If it's an in-person interaction:

Is the environment welcoming?_____

_____

_____

Is there background music? ☐ Yes ☐ No, If yes, what type of music? _____

_____

How would you describe the lighting?_____

_____

_____

What scents are present?_____

_____

How do patients feel in this environment?_____

_____

_____

What is the overall temperature?_____

_____

_____

Describe the employees' demeanor and attitude.

_____

_____

_____

_____

If it's a phone interaction:

How is the phone answered?_____

_____

_____

Is the greeting consistent for everyone? ☐ Yes ☐ No

Can the person who answers the phone directly assist the patient?
☐ Yes ☐ No (Please explain.) _____

_____

_____

How long does it typically take for the patient to reach someone
who can help them?_____

_____

_____

Examine the treatment patients receive throughout their interaction
with your practice. Create a comprehensive description of their ideal
experience.

_____

_____

_____

_____

_____

_____

_____

_____

_____

_____

_____

Organizational Personality: Unveiling Your Essence

Having identified your practices goals, values, mission, target audience, and the ideal patient and patient experience, it is now time to explore your practice's personality, attitude, and style.

Attitude: Consider how your practice's emotions, values, and beliefs manifest themselves in its overall demeanor. *Describe your practice's attitude.* _____

_____

_____

_____

_____

_____

Style: Explore both the visual aspects and the approach your practice takes in handling various matters. Visual style encompasses your practice's distinctive appearance, while the approach refers to the manner in which you conduct your operations. *Describe your practice's style, exploring both the visual and the manner in which your organization approaches things.* _____

_____

_____

_____

_____

_____

_____

_____

_____

_____

_____

Personality: Delve into the essence of your practice, examining areas such as your strengths, causes you support, interactions with employees, patients, vendors, and the general public, as well as the motivating factors that drive your practice. *Describe your practice's personality including what you are good at, causes that you support, interactions with employees, clients, vendors, the public in general, things that motive the practice, etc.*_____

_____

_____

_____

_____

_____

_____

_____

_____

_____

_____

_____

_____

_____

Organizational Voice: Harmonizing Your Communication

As you scrutinize your existing marketing materials, aim to identify and solidify the type of voice you want to convey through them. Your practice's voice emerges from a combination of attitude, tone, and personal style.

Maintain consistency between the voice used in your marketing materials and your interactions with patients. Consider your level of detail, descriptive language, use of colloquialisms or slang, and whether you prefer a formal or more informal tone. Developing the appropriate voice for your practice is crucial in creating a cohesive brand image.

Examine how your practice's attitude and personality shine through in its writing. Define the tone you aim to achieve and describe the personal style that reflects your practice's character. Analyze how these elements amalgamate to create your practice's distinctive voice. Additionally, identify any other crucial elements that must be communicated to ensure others can understand and replicate your desired voice when producing material for your practice.

_____

_____

_____

_____

_____

_____

_____

_____

_____

It's worth noting that your practice may have different variations of its voice when addressing different audience segments. However, all variations should be recognizable as the voice of your practice. For instance, you might adopt a more formal tone when interacting with prospects and a more informal tone for internal communications. Despite the differences, both styles of communication should still be identifiable as belonging to your practice.

If your practice has multiple facets to its voice, provide an explanation of how they manifest and in what contexts they are employed.

By addressing these aspects of your practice's identity, you will lay a solid foundation for crafting a compelling and engaging brand presence. Remember, the process of sculpting your practice's identity is not linear, and it may require periodic reassessment and adjustment as your practice evolves. Embrace this journey as an opportunity to grow and thrive.

CHAPTER 18

PLAYBOOK FOR A UNIFIED VOICE

In Playbook for a Unified Voice we will work on crafting a new brand standards handbook for your practice. With this document to you will lay the foundation for having all your communications and visuals being consistent and in-line with the new brand identity you have been developing over the past few chapters.

This chapter takes what you have developed and crafts a comprehensive brand guideline for your practice. Here you will spell out the specifications for how to use your logo. What typeface best reflects what you have learned about your practice. A description, and example of, your practices voice. Sample images that show the style of photography that should be used. Colors, and other graphic elements that should be used to help create consistency and easily recognition of your marketing pieces and or products.

Once you have completed this chapter download the Branding Standards Template PowerPoint from brandingyourpractice.com/downloads and start transferring your answers along with visual samples into the corresponding slides. This will provide you with a working brand standards document you can share with your practice.

Now, jump right in and get started creating the standards and guidelines your practice will use to keep your brand message on target and strong.

In this section we are going to work on compiling all the elements that you've worked on into more formal Brand Standards guideline, or a Brand Book.

Introduction & Background

Forward. When you are developing the forward for your branding guidelines it is a good idea to explain why you are looking to develop a system, especially if your practice has never previously had any type of formal branding standards. If you have, this is a wonderful opportunity to explain why there is a revision to, or a new system being developed.

Message from Your CEO / President. This needs to be a formal letter instructing the reader as to the importance of the new standards and guidelines that are being put into place and assure the reader that the management of the practice has put the full weight of their support behind this endeavor and making it a success. If you are the CEO / President take a moment to write out a letter. If you are not, you may want to take this section to write out the important topics that the CEO / President will need to know to write an effective letter.

Our Mission & Values. This section is just what it appears to be a place where you can state the mission and values of the practice that you developed in Chapter 17. As you are reviewing what you wrote in take this opportunity to clean up any text or grammar issues so that you have a polished version of your Mission,and Values to incorporate into your Brand Standards.

Our Brand. In Chapter 13 we identified our existing brand and in Chapter 17 we developed the structure for what we want our brand to be. Here is the perfect place to put all this information so that the reader comes to have an understanding of where you came from and where you are wanting to go. In this section, we can also place item such as competitive analysis, SWAT chart, and target audience personifications. All of this will allow for your reader to have a better understanding of what the practice is looking for when developing and rolling out the new brand. Write down that you want to include in this section, being sure to note any visuals (such as the SWAT chart, or examples of your competitors materials) that you want to include in this section of your Branding Standards.

_____

_____

What we stand for. This is a continuation of the last two topics and can include any information that you want that would fall under this heading. I find that this is a wonderful area for placing the company goals. As you have stated Our Mission & Values previously, and then expressed and overview of what you want from the brand in Our Brand, a statement of Goals would be perfect for What We Stand For". Write down what you want to include in this section of your Brand Standards and be sure to go back to the goals that you wrote in Chapter 17 and polish your statements.

_____

_____

The Role of Brand Identity.

Brand identity is the cement that holds these components together and provides a visual consistency and coherence to the outside. This is where we can assist our clients and the public in recognizing us with the way we present information, visually, audibly, and in writing. With consistency across the available media, it becomes comforting to the audience – they recognize and "know" us. And hopefully we become the "friend" that they look for when they are in the market for the products and services that we offer. This consistency allows for a sense of understanding and familiarity. Individuals like to engage with people and practices that they feel a connection with. Brand Identity allows for us to prove this through consistent application and tone in our dealings with our clients, potential clients and the public at large. Once major item to remember is that this must go across ALL aspects of the practice, not just the traditional identity packages of printed business materials.

Feel free to use the above or to write out a statement of your own on the importance of brand identity for your practice.

_____

_____

How to Use the Guidelines.

It is important for your practice to learn the correct utilization of these guidelines. If they don't use the guidelines that you have created then the effort that you have put into their development is pointless and an effort in futility. So first off you will need to express the importance of the guidelines (which hopefully the letter from the CEO/President has helped to do) and you have to provide them with strategies and understanding of how these should be used.

To that end, we need to establish WHO will be using these guidelines. For the most ideal situation you will have a small contingent that will be responsible for the direct creation of elements for your practice who have this as their handbook to ensure that all pieces are in compliance and then roll them out to the rest of the practice. However, depending on the size of your practice that may not be feasible, so you need to provide structure to everyone who may have a reason to utilize the practice logo or create marketing, display pieces or advertising.

Branding guidelines will be used by internal employees (management, marketing, communications, design, legal, sales, web gurus, human resources, PR, product designers, anyone creating presentations, customer service) and external partners (branding firms, design firms, advertising agencies, information architects, technologists, packaging design firms, architects, writers, co-branding partners).

For this group, you need them to have easy access to the manual and it needs to be clear what IS acceptable, as well as what IS NOT acceptable for the practice.

If you need the practices logo – you will download it from the branding site or request from the authorized resource.

Elements provided are not be to be stretched, skewed, squashed or manipulated in any way that does not keep them in the proper prospective. Color are provided in CMYK, RGB, and Hexadecimal. These are the approved colors and should be used in all materials. If you do not know how to set a color in the program that you are using you can download a HOW TO from (URL) or request assistance from (name / department / email address).

These guidelines are to be utilized for the creation of all materials both internal and externally facing for the practice. Please utilize the templates that have been provided, or if no template exists the final product should comply with all specifications located within the guidelines. Please direct any questions to (name / department / email address).

If you are unsure if the piece that has been create complies with all of the practices branding protocol, please send a copy to (name / department / email address) for review and approval before rolling out to the public or employees.

Thank you for your assistance in maintain our practices branding.

Using the above as starting point write out instructions for how your practices branding guidelines should be used.

_____

_____

Brand Identity Elements

Your logo may be comprised of both a brandmark and a logotype. Some practice have dropped their logotypes because their symbols have become recognizable on their own. You need to make a determination if your brandmark/logotype can be used without the other. If they can, under what circumstances is this permissible.

Brandmark

The brandmark is the wordmark, letterform, symbol, emblem, pictorial mark that is in your logo. Your logo may also have a logotype which is the type element of your logo. This can become a little confusing as there are logos who's brandmarks are stylized text such as Google, Dell, and IBM. This graphical element of text is considered a brand mark even through it is textual in nature.

Logotype

Logotype is a bit more straight forward in that it is the actual text of the logo. The word, or words, in a specific font which may or may not be modified or redrawn from their original format.

Tagline

Does your practice have a tagline? If not, should you?

A tagline is a short phrase that is carefully designed to influence customers buying behaviors by causing an emotion response while capturing the practices personality and positioning. Taglines help to differentiate you from your competition and help to share the essence of your practices brand.

If you have a tagline write it here:

_____

Does it reflect your practices brand essence? It's personality? Does it evoke an emotional response? If Yes - great! If No, take a moment to brainstorm taglines that would be more in line with the new brand that you are developing.

_____

_____

Is there a specific typeface, size, color, or position that your tagline should always appear in? _____

_____

Signature

When you incorporate your tagline into your logo you are developing a "Signature". A signature is comprised of your brandmark, logotype and tagline. However, a logo (brandmark & logotype) can also be referred to as a signature without including a tagline.

Now that we've gone over these elements it's time for you to put this knowledge into action and take your existing logo / signature and identify the various element that make up your practices mark.

Identify the Signature, Brandmark & Logotype in your practice mark in the space below. Don't worry about being an artist, this important part is to be able to identify the element and understand how they work together, and if you want to allow any of them to be used on their own.

Name in Text

How do you want your practice name to be written in text? _

_____

Do you want your practice name written out only the first reference or each and every time? _____

_____

Is there an abbreviation that is acceptable to be used? _____

_____

Are their special circumstances for a different usage?_____

_____

Incorrect Usage of Elements

Here you can specify some ways that your logo / signature / tagline may be used that you DON'T want done.

Here are a few suggestions:

Do you want your brandmark used separately from your logotype? (If yes, are there specific ways you want it used / not used? If no, clearly state that.) _____

_____

Can the colors be changes? _____

_____

Can the typeface be changes? _____

_____

_____

What about skewing, squashing, or stretching? _____

_____

The white space surrounding your logo is as important as your logo itself. If you allow your logo to have other elements too close, it looses it's distinction and importance. If you're logo did not come with some basic specification, this is your opportunity to establish some basic standards. Often times an element from the logo itself is used as a measuring device for surrounding white space.

_____

_____

Nomenclature

Communicative vs. Legal Names

What is your practices formal (legal) and informal (communicative) name? _____

_____

_____

When should each of these names be used? _____

_____

_____

_____

Corporate

Is there any type of special demarcation for reference to your practices corporate office? If so, what is it and how should it be denoted? _____

_____

_____

_____

Division

Is there any type of special demarcation for reference to your practices divisions? If so, what is it and how should they be denoted? _____

_____

_____

Business Unit

Is there any type of special demarcation for reference to your practices business units? If so, what is it and how should they be denoted? _____

_____

_____

Product and Service Trademarks

Is there any type of special demarcation for reference to your practices product and service trademarks? If so, what are they and how should they be denoted? _____

_____

Naming Guidelines and Strategy

What are the processes used to develop and select every name candidate?_____

What are the standard deciding criteria that all names are evaluated against?_____

What elements of each name should related to the product or services vs the elements that should relate back to the practices brand?_____

_____

What conventions or guides are used in your naming architecture?_

_____

When you are naming a product or service are you ensuring that the brand message is relayed consistency and reflective of the practices core values? ☐ Yes ☐ No

Does the name provide tone / imagery that supports the values of the brand within the consumers consciousness? ☐ Yes ☐ No

Is there a hierarchy to your naming conventions? *(How names are applied to different tiers, sub-brands, classes, etc.?)* ☐ Yes ☐ No

Is there a consistent way that names are developed? *(Consistently descriptive? Consistently coined?)* ☐ Yes ☐ No

Are the brands names structurally similar? *(e.g. Apple's i-convention)* ☐ Yes ☐ No

Do all of the names have similar Linguistic or orthographic

similarities? ☐ Yes ☐ No

Does your practice have a strategy established for naming products/services? ☐ Yes ☐ No If yes, what is the strategy for using names to advance the brand? _____

_____

_____

Now that you have a brand wide pre-defined guideline for naming products and services you need to implement it across your practice. Keep in mid the following three facets of naming:

> PERCEPTION - How is the name perceived, understood and embraced as a branding opportunity withing the practice

> PRACTICE - Best practices for how naming is undertaken within the practice

> PRODUCT - How the names come to life and work together within the practice.

Proper naming takes time and diligence, but the return help to move forward your branding effort more clearly and consistently at every touch point.

Color

Color is a critical part of your brand identity. Color incites emotional response and is memorable. You want to establish a color system for your practice that allows your client to have confidence that they are working with you. They recognize your logo, your colors and your voice. Consistency in your color usage across all of your materials and media applications allows for this assurance.

Color consistency can be a tricky issue however. colors come in a variety of formats based on their presentation. For print colors we need to look at CMKY (Cyan Magenta Black Yellow) or Spot Colors (colors that are specially blended - Pantone PMS colors are spot colors). CMYK colors are based on percentages of each color, so your numbers will range from 0–100%. If you are working with display (web/video) your colors need to be RGB (Red Green Blue). RGB color utilize a scale from 0 to 255 (the scale is set in relations to bytes), where 0 means not used and 255 is 100%. However you must remember that when dealing with print (CMYK)100% of all colors gives you BLACK, in working with displays where you use light waves (RGB)100% of each color gives you WHITE. You may also uses hexadecimal codes for colors which contains information for RGB representing each color by a two digit alpha-numeric code from 0-9, A-F (A-F = 10-15). On screen colors also suffer from inconsistency across platform, system calibration differences, and variations of the displays they are see on.

You need to have both the CMYK and the RGB values for all of the colors that you specify.

You should also be aware that colors emotional response and perception can vary greatly when you are dealing with individuals from different countries or ethnicities. Make sure you check your color selection against your target audiences color perceptions. You don't want to be using a color that they find incongruent with the message that you are wanting to portray.

You my have as many or as few colors in each of these systems as you want. I have provided 4 slots, but you do not have to use them all, or be limited by that number.

Brand Color System

The first stop in your path to standardized colors is your logo. These are the foundations of your brand colors. Look at your logo right now and determine how many colors your logo has. Do you know the color's RGB/CMYK numbers? If not you can upload your logo to *http://www.ginifab.com/feeds/pms/pms_color_in_image.php* and have the RGB/CMYK & suggested Pantone color identified when you roll over the different areas of your logo.

Color _____

    R _____ G _____ B _____

    C _____ M _____ Y _____ K _____

    Pantone _____

    HEXCode: _____

Color _____

    R _____ G _____ B _____

    C _____ M _____ Y _____ K _____

    Pantone _____

    HEXCode: _____

Color _____

    R _____ G _____ B _____

    C _____ M _____ Y _____ K _____

    Pantone _____

    HEXCode: _____

Color _____

    R _____ G _____ B _____

    C _____ M _____ Y _____ K _____

    Pantone _____

    HEXCode: _____

Default Color System

These are the main colors that your practice will be utilizing. These colors may be your brand colors, or they may be a collection of colors that are to be used in place of / addition to your logo colors. *(Note: Your logo colors should NEVER change unless you have a VERY specific reason & strategy behind this.)*

Color _____

    R _____ G _____ B _____

    C _____ M _____ Y _____ K _____

    Pantone _____

    HEXCode: _____

Color _____

    R _____ G _____ B _____

    C _____ M _____ Y _____ K _____

    Pantone _____

    HEXCode: _____

Color _____

    R _____ G _____ B _____

    C _____ M _____ Y _____ K _____

    Pantone _____

    HEXCode: _____

Color _____

    R _____ G _____ B _____

    C _____ M _____ Y _____ K _____

    Pantone _____

    HEXCode: _____

Color _____

    R _____ G _____ B _____

    C _____ M _____ Y _____ K _____

    Pantone _____

    HEXCode: _____

Color _____

    R _____ G _____ B _____

    C _____ M _____ Y _____ K _____

    Pantone _____

    HEXCode: _____

Supporting Color System

These are secondary colors. These colors may be used for contrasting or highlighted against the default / brand colors. You do not have to have supporting colors.

Color _____   Color _____

   R _____ G _____ B _____   R _____ G _____ B _____

   C _____ M _____ Y _____ K _____   C _____ M _____ Y _____ K _____

   Pantone _____   Pantone _____

   HEXCode: _____   HEXCode: _____

Color _____   Color _____

   R _____ G _____ B _____   R _____ G _____ B _____

   C _____ M _____ Y _____ K _____   C _____ M _____ Y _____ K _____

   Pantone _____   Pantone _____

   HEXCode: _____   HEXCode: _____

Signature Color System

Generally these are the same as your brand color systems. However, you may have variation if you have color differentiators for divisions, departments, business units, etc. If you do have variations be sure to clearly explain when and how they are to be used.

Color _____   Color _____

   R _____ G _____ B _____   R _____ G _____ B _____

   C _____ M _____ Y _____ K _____   C _____ M _____ Y _____ K _____

   Pantone _____   Pantone _____

   HEXCode: _____   HEXCode: _____

Color _____   Color _____

   R _____ G _____ B _____   R _____ G _____ B _____

   C _____ M _____ Y _____ K _____   C _____ M _____ Y _____ K _____

   Pantone _____   Pantone _____

   HEXCode: _____   HEXCode: _____

Explanation: _____

_____

_____

_____

_____

Incorrect Use of Color

You need to provide examples of incorrect color usage for your practice. For example you may show the logo in inappropriate colors. You may have colors that should NEVER be used that you want to call out as specific example of what NOT to do. You may want to provide example of materials using the colors incorrectly so that how they should be used become more clearly expressed.

Take a few minutes and think about how your colors could be used in a manner that would not support your brand / practiceal goals. Write those below. If you want to include examples, write those down as well, so you can have the incorrect images created to include in your guidelines.

_____

_____

Signatures / Logos

Corporate Signature

This is the main signature / logo for the practice. All practice have a corporate signature. You may not have variations, subsidiary, or product signatures, but if you have a logo you have a corporate signature.

What is your corporate signature?

_____

_____

_____

Signature Variations

As I stated above, you may not have variation. A common example is if you have a stacked logo, you have a horizontal one as well, If your practice does this then you have variations. It is also common for practice to have their logos in full color, black, gray scale, and white as these open greater opportunities for better viability, and/or reduced printing cost.

What variations do you have?

_____

_____

Incorrect Signature Usage

How can your corporate signature be used incorrectly? This is where you explain incorrect coloring, skewing, stretching, squishing, using with the wrong background colors, or on a busy background, or using the wrong variation of the logo.

Take a moment to think about how your logo could be distorted, or used in a manner that doesn't adhere to how you want your brand represented. Write these down.

_____

_____

_____

Subsidiary Signatures

Does your practice have subsidiaries? If so, how do you want your signature represented? Is it just the subsidiary signature or will it be displayed jointly with the corporate signature? How will they be positioned in relation to one another? Is there a size difference? Are the subsidiaries signatures modifications of the corporate? How so?

_____

_____

Product Signatures

Does your practice have products or services that are branded? Is just the product or service signature displayed or will it be displayed jointly with the corporate signature? How will they be positioned in relation to one another? Is there a size difference?

_____

_____

Signature with Tagline

Here you will want to place your logo with your tagline (if you have one) attached and any variations of this version of the signature.

Can your tagline be placed in a location not attached to the logo? Specify when the signature with the tagline should be used, and when the logo with out the tagline should be used. Can the tagline be used separate from the logo. What are the specification for it's use separately?

_____

_____

Incorrect Tagline Treatment

What are the inappropriate usages of your tagline?

_____

_____

Clear Space Around Signature

The white space surrounding your logo is as important as your logo itself. If you allow your logo to have other elements too close, it looses it's distinction and importance. If you're logo did not come with some basic specification, this is your opportunity to establish some basic standards. Often times an element from the logo itself is used as a measuring device for surrounding white space.

If you have alternate signatures, you will need to make sure they all have clear space set. You may also want to establish specifications for specific uses such as email signatures where the left margin may need to be altered to allow for alignment within the email.

_____

_____

_____

Signature Size

You will want to set a minimum size for the use of your logo. You want to make sure that the minimum size that the logo is used at still allows for it to be clearly read. If your logo is in vector format (AI, EPS) you will be able to scale it from very small to very large without the loss of any resolution. If you are working with bitmap (PNG, JPG) formats you will need to have multiple files at the appropriate sized to ensure quality resolution of your practices signature.

What is the minimum size of your logo? _____

_____

What is the maximum size you anticipate regularly using your logo at? _____

_____

What other sizes will you need your logo at? _____

_____

You will need to have your logo in all of these sized. For web/digital use you will need to have your logo in RGB format and in CMYK for print use. JPG files have a solid background (typically white), if you need a transparent background you will want PNG files.

Typography

You will want to establish consistent typography across your materials. To do this you will need to select typefaces (fonts) that will be used in all of your materials. You may have primary "organizational" typefaces that are used in your official communications and marketing materials, as well as secondary typefaces that are more common (built into your operating system) to ensure that all of your practices employees are able to utilize an approve typeface in their letters and emails.

Please remember typefaces are licensed pieces of software. You must have a license for every system that is utilizing a font. A font is a single typeface at a specific weight, so for example, if you are using Arial Regular, Bold, Italic, Bold Italic - this is actually 4 fonts. The more variation a typeface has, the larger number of fonts are used. When you are purchasing licenses for fonts you are purchasing the right to use a specific font and weight not all of the weights that may be available. There are many times discounts if you buy a collection of fonts (multiple weights) within the same typeface. The price for a typeface varies widely from "free" to $100's per each font. You will also need to make sure you are purchasing enough seats for all of the individuals who will need access to the typeface.

There are a large number of foundries that sell typefaces. Some of the most common are: fonts.com, myfont.com, typekit.com, dafont. com (not a foundry but does allow you explore many fonts and links you to where you can purchase, some are free but be sure to check if it is for personal or business use) A more comprehensive list will be at the end of this book.

Typeface Family

What is the typeface (collection of fonts) that you want to utilized for the primary communications for your practice. This would be the typeface that would be used in your stationary and marketing materials. What weights (regular, italic, book, book italic, medium, medium italic, semi-bold, semi-bold italic, bold, bold italic, black,

black italic, etc) do you need?

_____

_____

_____

Supporting Typefaces

Are there secondary typefaces that may be used?

_____

_____

Special Displace Faces

Do you want to identify special typefaces for use in banners, posters and other displays? Is there any other special circumstance that you want to have a special font for?

_____

_____

Typeface for Word Processing

Do you want to specify a common system font for use by your general staff to reduce the typography expense and technical support needed to install the custom typeface onto all of your systems?

_____

_____

Application Standards and Templates

What types of standards and templates do you need for the following topics. Please note you will need to either create these standards and templates yourself, or hire someone to do them for you. It is also ideal that you have the specifications all of your main documents written down to ensure they can be recreated if the original templates are lost or become damaged.

U.S. Business Papers

- ☐ Corporate letterhead
- ☐ Typing template
- ☐ Division letterhead
- ☐ Personalized letterhead
- ☐ Second sheet
- ☐ Envelopes #10
- ☐ Monarch letterhead
- ☐ Monarch envelopes
- ☐ Memo templates
- ☐ Business cards - corporate
- ☐ Business cards - sale
- ☐ Fax (electronic) template

- ☐ Notepads
- ☐ News releases
- ☐ Mailing labels
- ☐ Window envelope
- ☐ Large mailing envelope
- ☐ Mailing label
- ☐ Announcements
- ☐ Thank you cards
- ☐ Invitations
- ☐ CD labels
- ☐ _____
- ☐ _____
- ☐ _____

International Business Papers

- ☐ A-4 letterhead
- ☐ A-4 personalized letterhead
- ☐ A-4 business envelope

- ☐ Business cards
- ☐ _____
- ☐ _____

Digital Media

- ☐ Website
- ☐ Internet
- ☐ Extranet
- ☐ Blogs
- ☐ Architecture
- ☐ Style guides
- ☐ Interface

- ☐ Content
- ☐ Color
- ☐ Typefaces
- ☐ Imagery
- ☐ Sound
- ☐ _____
- ☐ _____

Forms

- ☐ Form elements
- ☐ Vertical and horizontal
- ☐ Form grid
- ☐ Purchase order
- ☐ Invoice
- ☐ Shipping

- ☐ _____
- ☐ _____
- ☐ _____
- ☐ _____
- ☐ _____
- ☐ _____

Marketing Materials

- ☐ Voice and tone
- ☐ Imagery
- ☐ Signature placement
- ☐ Folder
- ☐ Covers
- ☐ Recommended grids
- ☐ Brochure system, var sizes
- ☐ Mastheads
- ☐ Product sheets
- ☐ Direct mail
- ☐ Newsletters
- ☐ Posters
- ☐ Postcards
- ☐ _____
- ☐ _____

Advertising

- ☐ Advertising signatures
- ☐ Tagline usage
- ☐ Signature placement on ads
- ☐ Typography
- ☐ Television advertising grid
- ☐ _____

Presentation & Proposals

- ☐ Vertical covers
- ☐ Horizontal covers
- ☐ Covers with windows
- ☐ Interior grid
- ☐ PowerPoint templates
- ☐ PowerPoint imagery
- ☐ _____
- ☐ _____

Exhibits

- ☐ Trade show booth
- ☐ Banners
- ☐ Point of purchase
- ☐ Table top displays
- ☐ Name tags
- ☐ _____

Signage

- ☐ External signage
- ☐ Internal signage
- ☐ Color
- ☐ Typography
- ☐ Materials and finishes
- ☐ Lighting considerations
- ☐ Fabrication guidelines
- ☐ Company flag
- ☐ _____
- ☐ _____

Vehicle Identification

- ☐ Vans
- ☐ Cars
- ☐ Buses
- ☐ Planes
- ☐ Trucks
- ☐ _____

Packaging

☐ Legal considerations	☐ Boxes
☐ Package Sizes	☐ Bags
☐ Package grids	☐ Cartons
☐ Product Signatures	☐ _____
☐ Labeling system	☐ _____

Uniforms

☐ Winter	☐ Rain gear
☐ Spring	☐ _____
☐ Summer	☐ _____
☐ Fall	☐ _____

Ephemera

☐ Golf shirt	☐ Golf balls
☐ Baseball caps	☐ Memo cubes
☐ Ties	☐ Mouse pads
☐ Portfolios	☐ Customer store website
☐ Pens	☐ Key chains
☐ Umbrellas	☐ Koozies
☐ Mugs	☐ _____
☐ Pins	☐ _____
☐ Scarves	☐ _____

Resources

A comprehensive brand standard guide benefits from having a reference section that provides the end user information about where to find the following items, or who to contact for additional information.

Image Library

☐ Photography	☐ Illustration

Reproduction Files

☐ Brandmark only	☐ Signature (black)
☐ Signature (full-color)	☐ Signature (white)
☐ Signature (one-color)	☐ Signature (vector)

☐ PC   ☐ _____
☐ Mac   ☐ _____

Miscellaneous
☐ Who to contact with   ☐ Design inquiries
   questions   ☐ Clearance process
☐ Frequently asked   ☐ Legal information
   questions   ☐ Ordering information

CHAPTER 19

TOUCHPOINTS

Touchpoints are the individual items/events/or experiences that an individual has with your practice. This can be anything from your business card or brochure to meeting with you at an event. If you sell products, they are touchpoints, both when a prospective patients view them on the shelf and once they have been purchased and used. Take a few moments and use the worksheet (see Appendix E or download from brandingyourpractice.com/downloads) to identify the touchpoints of your business.

Once you have checked them off or added them to the list, evaluate how your patient interacts with each one. Does each of the touchpoints further your brand message? Are they fulfilling a need for your prospect/client?

Here are some examples to get you started.

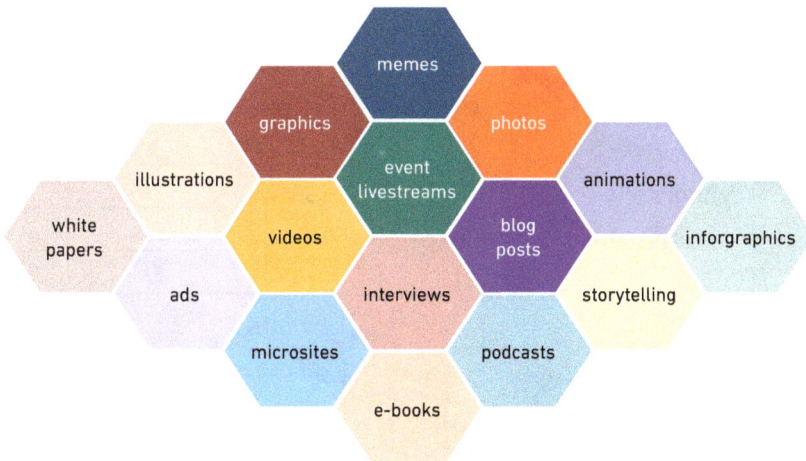

- advertising
- app icons
- brand initiatives
- collateral
- ephemera
- packaging

- product design
- signage
- stationery
- uniforms
- vehicles
- website

TOUCHPOINTS

- [ ] U.S. Business Papers
  - [ ] Corporate Letterhead
  - [ ] #10 Envelopes
  - [ ] Business Cards
  - [ ] CD Labels
  - [ ] Forms
    - [ ] Check-in
    - [ ] _____
    - [ ] _____
    - [ ] _____
    - [ ] _____
    - [ ] _____
  - [ ] Proposals
- [ ] Digital Media - Mobile
  - [ ] Website
  - [ ] Intranet
  - [ ] Blogs
  - [ ] Color
  - [ ] Content
  - [ ] Interface
  - [ ] Typography
  - [ ] Imagery
  - [ ] Sound
  - [ ] Emails
  - [ ] Apps
  - [ ] Social Networks
- [ ] Marketing Materials
  - [ ] Imagery
  - [ ] Signature Placement
  - [ ] Covers
  - [ ] Brochure System
  - [ ] Masthead
  - [ ] Product Sheets

- [ ] Newsletters
- [ ] Presentations
- [ ] Publications
- [ ] Pre-Appt Package
- [ ] VIP Matchbook Package
- [ ] Postcards
- [ ] Advertising
  - [ ] Sales Promotions
  - [ ] Direct Mail
  - [ ] Billboards
  - [ ] Articles
  - [ ] Magazine Tear Sheets
  - [ ] Bus Shelters
  - [ ] _____
  - [ ] _____
- [ ] Presentation & Proposals
  - [ ] Vertical Covers
  - [ ] PowerPoint Templates
  - [ ] PowerPoint Imagery
  - [ ] _____
  - [ ] _____
  - [ ] _____
  - [ ] _____
- [ ] Exhibits
  - [ ] Trade Show Booths
  - [ ] Banners
  - [ ] Name Tags
  - [ ] Signage
- [ ] Signage
  - [ ] External Signage
  - [ ] Internal Signage
  - [ ] Color
  - [ ] Typography

- ☐ Fabrication Guidelines
- ☐ Packaging - Product
  - ☐ Packaging Size
  - ☐ Product Signatures
  - ☐ Labeling Systems
  - ☐ Packaging Artwork
- ☐ Uniforms
  - ☐ Shirts
  - ☐ Jackets
  - ☐ Hats
  - ☐ Bags
- ☐ Ephemera
  - ☐ Golf shirts
  - ☐ Baseball caps
  - ☐ Portfolios
  - ☐ Pens
  - ☐ Mugs
- ☐ Audio
  - ☐ Speeches
  - ☐ Video
    - ☐ Intro graphics
    - ☐ Lower Thirds
    - ☐ Transitions
    - ☐ Credit Scroll
  - ☐ Podcast
    - ☐ Page Graphics
    - ☐ Series Artwork
  - ☐ Word of Mouth
  - ☐ Voicemails
  - ☐ Radio Spots
- ☐ _____
- ☐ _____
- ☐ _____
- ☐ _____

- ☐ _____
- ☐ _____
- ☐ _____
- ☐ Environments
  - ☐ Wall color
  - ☐ Music
  - ☐ Lighting
  - ☐ Smell
- ☐ Vehicles
  - ☐ Color
  - ☐ Vehicle wraps
  - ☐ Logo Magnets
- ☐ Experiences
  - ☐ Check-in
  - ☐ Intake/transition to exam room
  - ☐ Appt Confirmation - Call
  - ☐ Appt Confirmation - SMS
- ☐ Public Relations
- ☐ Services
- ☐ Employees
- ☐ _____
- ☐ _____
- ☐ _____
- ☐ _____
- ☐ _____
- ☐ _____
- ☐ _____
- ☐ _____
- ☐ _____
- ☐ _____
- ☐ _____
- ☐ _____

Think about all of the way's that you interact with prospects and customers. Each of these contribute to the collective awareness of your brand. This list is not comprehensive, so please add items or occurrences of interactions. Review each of these elements for alignment with your brand purpose, values, and story.

How do our organizations materials compare to our competitors?

_____

_____

_____

Are we saying the same thing?

_____

_____

_____

Can you tell our material from the competitors by the way the copy is written? Or is it interchangeable?

_____

_____

_____

Do our materials all use the same color pallet?

_____

_____

_____

Is the logo (if you have one) used consistently across all pieces?

_____

_____

_____

Do the images selected have a similar feel? Is the style consistent?

_____

_____

_____

Do the images that we use support what is being said or are they contradicting each other?

_____

_____

Was color selection made consciously?

_____

_____

Is the meaning and impact of our color chose understood for each of our markets? If we engage with international clients, have we considered our color selection in relation to their culture?

_____

_____

_____

_____

PART 4

Internal Branding & Culture

"The conversation will be about one community working together to achieve a single purpose. And when a business's control over these sometimes-paid roles is tentative at best, the best tool we have is culture."

— Josh Levine
author *Great Mondays*

Josh Levine is a renowned author, speaker, and consultant specializing in company culture and employee experience. He is the founder and CEO of Great Mondays, a consultancy focused on helping organizations design and implement exceptional company cultures. Levine has worked with numerous well-known companies, including Airbnb, Nike, and Marvel, to transform their cultures and create environments where employees thrive. He is also the author of "Great Mondays: How to Design a Company Culture Employees Love," which provides practical insights and strategies for creating a positive and engaging workplace culture. With his expertise and passion for organizational culture, Josh Levine has become a respected thought leader in the field.

CHAPTER 20

FOUNDATIONS FOR INTERNAL COMMUNICATIONS

Your internal branding is built upon the work that we have already completed in the first three sections of this program. Here we take the Purpose, Vision, Values, Personality, Promise, and Positioning and develop the strategy to communicate these to the internal staff of the company. Our goal is to create buy-in with our employees and to create an environment (culture) that will continue to support and perpetuate the application of these principles across the organization. It is here that the authenticity of our brand is born, or destroyed.

It is through the development of an internal culture blueprint and it's dissemination throughout with internal communications, policies and procedures that we can create a living breathing culture within the organization that is reflective of the vision and values that the organization professes to hold dear.

Remember, as we've covered before, authenticity is paramount in branding. Inauthentic brands are quickly reveled and loose not only their reputation with their employees, but eventually with their clients and their market shares.

By the end of Part 4 you will have an understanding of what it takes to manage the internal communications of an organization, as well as

The Communication Process

Agree/Own the Message
Target/Tailor/Test

Feedback:

— surveys

— focus groups

50% of communication is listening

100% of communication is ownership

Deliver:

— face-to-face (primary)

— publications (secondary)

develop the process for on-boarding employees, having them buy-in to the new brand, and created benchmarks to aid the adherence to the values and culture that you are working to develop.

Let's start of by examining the Foundational elements of our brand. Review the previous chapters and write out the following:

Purpose: _____

_____

Vision: _____

_____

Values (See Page 91): _____

_____

Personality (See Page 97): _____

_____

Promise: _____

_____

Positioning: _____

_____

Internal Communication Strategy

Let's start our exploration with the options that we have in communicating our brands central elements to our employees, internal staff & vendors who may support us with communication and marketing efforts.

By applying the principles of consumer advertising to internal communications, you as a leader of your organization can guide employees to a better understanding of the brand vision. Applying these principles enables employees to "live" the vision in their day-to-day activities. And when employees live that vision, customers are much more likely to experience the company in a way that's consistent with what you've promised.

Company wide presentation/roll-out

One option is to create an event for the entire company.

1. Choose your time - Look for a natural turning point. A time of change, or challenge when employees are seeking direction and will respond receptively to the initiatives.

2. Link Internal and External Marketing - Have consistency between your internal and external communications.

3. Bring the Brand Alive for Employees - You also want to create an emotional connection to inform the way they approach their jobs, even if they don't interact with customers. You want them to have the brand vision in their minds and to consider whether or not they are supporting the brand in every decision they make.

   a. Create a campaign to introduce and explain your brand message(s)

   b. Incorporate your message(s) into employee directed touch-points that are utilized in the day-to-day interactions

   c. Develop communication strategies designed to convince your employees of the merits and credibility of your brand

   d. Internal research - brand, mythos, folklore

   e. Materials must ring true for employees & draw on the company's very soul, reflecting & reinforcing what people care about

   f. Empower employees to deliver on brand promises (and marketing campaigns)

   g. Materials must be free of jargon & grandstanding - focus on the essence of the company

h. Materials must be creative & eye-catching (just like those delivered to external audience)

i. Communicate at a personal level (don't take the short cut of memos, videos or packages of materials) use rich medias

j. Feedback & participation from the target audience

Reinforce the brand - continuously

Checklist:
- [ ] Develop launch messages & new branded marketing assets
- [ ] Plan internal launch event
- [ ] Update all print & electronic materials
- [ ] Develop public relations strategy
- [ ] Get communication channels ready
- [ ] Conduct brand champion training
- [ ] Develop a save-the-date teaser campaign
- [ ] Prepare pre-launch communications
- [ ] Brainstorm on-brand employee gifts
- [ ] Order branded swag
- [ ] Internal brand engagement & education
- [ ] Employee on-boarding (brand training)
- [ ] Annual brand audit

What are Internal Communications?

Simply put internal communications are the messages that are shared within an organization to it's employees. Good internal communications is a two way street in which not only does the management send out communications, but they are receptive to receiving feedback from their employees.

Setting the Foundations

First and foremost managing internal communications is not a commonplace skill that anyone can just assume the duty of and succeed. Internal communications needs to be held in the domain of an in-house team or select trained individual, and requires a strategic foundation to ensure that those communications will be cohesive and engaging.

Over the decades internal communication has transitioned from the domain of just events and people to the sharing of corporate goals. Internal communication needs to be championed from the very top

> *"Smaller organizational decisions should be taken by senior individuals, but large ones should be decided as a group. Everyone's voice must be heard to avoid murmurs and back-biting."*
>
> **- St. Benedict,
> a 6th century monk**

of the organization and should be recognized as the responsibility of everyone from the CEO to line manager and supervisor. Organizations need their employees to understand what is expected of them and internal communication helps to deliver this.

These are some of the responsibilities that may fall to your internal communication representative:

- [ ] changing communications;
- [ ] communicating strategy;
- [ ] design and process of communication structures including feedback;
- [ ] developing the intranet;
- [ ] driving employee engagement;
- [ ] internalizing the brand;
- [ ] knowledge sharing;

Skills for Internal Communicators

If you are looking to hire an internal communicator the following is a list of skills that are necessary or beneficial to succeed at the task.

- [ ] business awareness/ literacy;
- [ ] business/financial literacy;
- [ ] business knowledge;
- [ ] understanding customer focus;
- [ ] communication coaching for line managers;
- [ ] consultancy skills;
- [ ] creativity;
- [ ] creative communication
- [ ] skills;
- [ ] diplomacy;
- [ ] e-communication development;
- [ ] facilitation skills;
- [ ] influencing and negotiation;
- [ ] internal branding and corporate branding;
- [ ] leadership communication and behaviors;
- [ ] listening skills;

- [ ] media management;
- [ ] organizational change/ change management;
- [ ] organizational development;
- [ ] passion and drive;
- [ ] political skills;
- [ ] process/best practice;
- [ ] psychology of communication;
- [ ] relationship building/ networking;

- [ ] resilience and tenacity;
- [ ] staying power and self-belief;
- [ ] strategic insight;
- [ ] strategic thinking ability;
- [ ] training, coaching, consulting;
- [ ] understanding the business;
- [ ] writing and presentation skills;

Who in your organization will be responsible for Internal Communications?

- [ ] Internal Communication Department
- [ ] Public Relations/Corporate Communications
- [ ] Human Resources

- [ ] Marketing
- [ ] IT & Knowledge Management
- [ ] Other: _____

_____

Determining the structure of your internal communication team.

How will you internal communication team be set up? Depending on the size of your organization this can be 1-2 people, or a multi-departmental team. One key factor to remember is that regardless of how big your organization is, it is imperative that you have buy-in from management and that you have a procedure in place that encourages two way communication.

Management Representative: _____

_____

Primary Internal Communication party(ies): _____

_____

Secondary Internal Communication members:_____

Brand Champions: _____

_____

These individuals/groups will make up your internal communication team. Be sure that everyone on this list understands what their responsibility will be in carrying out internal communications and supporting your internal brand and culture.

What type of organizational communication culture do you have?
☐ Power culture (centered on the founder)
☐ Role culture (emphasis on function and specialism. It has many procedures and rules. Job descriptions are prevalent here as are procedures for doing things and rules for settling disputes.)
☐ Person culture (The focus is on the individuals themselves as separate individuals who choose to work together. Where this kind of group has sprung up within universities and healthcare settings there can be real stresses and strains with the overarching structure, which will often be largely bureaucratic.)
☐ Task culture (focused on the job in hand or the project)

Building Your Internal Communication Strategy

A. Set Strategic Communication Goals
Identify business objectives.

1. _____

_____

2. _____

_____

3. _____

_____

Describe communication challenges for each objective.

1. _____

   _____

2. _____

   _____

3. _____

   _____

Define S.M.A.R.T. goals.

S	**Specific**	What will be accomplished? What actions will you take?
M	**Measurable**	What data will measure the goal? (How much? How well?
A	**Achievable**	Is the goal doable? Do you have the necessary skills and resources?
R	**Relevant**	How does the goal align with broader goals? Why is the result important?
T	**Time-Bound**	What is the time frame for accomplishing the goal?

1. _____

   _____

2. _____

   _____

3. _____

   _____

Define Your KPIs (Key Performance Indicators)

As you go threw the process of developing your KPIs keep in mind the four types that you will work with.

Strategic: These big-picture key performance indicators monitor organizational goals. Executives typically look to one or two strategic KPIs to find out how the organization is doing at any given time. Examples include return on investment, revenue and market share.

Operational: These KPIs typically measure performance in a shorter time frame, and are focused on organizational processes and efficiencies. Some examples include sales by region, average monthly transportation costs and cost per acquisition (CPA).

Functional Unit: Many key performance indicators are tied to specific functions, such finance or IT. While IT might track time to resolution or average uptime, finance KPIs track gross profit margin or return on assets. These functional KPIs can also be classified as strategic or operational.

Leading vs Lagging: Regardless of the type of key performance indicator you define, you should know the difference between leading indicators and lagging indicators. While leading KPIs can help predict outcomes, lagging KPIs track what has already happened. Organizations use a mix of both to ensure they're tracking what's most important

Define a quantifiable measure of performance (over time) for each strategic goal identified.

1. _____

_____

Type of KPI _____

_____

2. _____

_____

Type of KPI _____

_____

3. _____

_____

Type of KPI _____

_____

Assess the Audience

Who is your audience?

☐ Front-line staff   ☐ Supervisors/Line managers
☐ Board/Director   ☐ Voluntary Sector (non-
☐ Board/Director Senior   profits) Trustees, Volunteers,
   Management/Middle   Members
   Management

Be prepared to segment your audience along a range of less obvious permutations – age, gender, race, disability, etc. Do you need to segment your audience? ☐ Yes ☐ No

If Yes, how? _____

_____

What level of influence do each of the segments identified have within the organization?

_____

_____

Blocks to communication that need to be taken into consideration:

☐ age   ☐ overactive   ☐ too much of the
☐ gender   grapevine   same old thing
☐ disability   ☐ previous history   ☐ remote workers
☐ culture/religion   of organization   ☐ regional
☐ channel   ☐ distrust in   differences.
   distortions   management

Key Points to Consider:

- ☐ Take into account the feelings of all sections of the workforce – look particularly for resentment.
- ☐ Cultural diversity could be seen as an opportunity rather than an extra burden on resources.
- ☐ Consider quality of paper, size of typeface, use of color when communicating with audiences with disabilities or from a different cultural background.
- ☐ Interpreters are useful in group meetings for people with hearing difficulties but also those who may not speak good English.
- ☐ Dispersed teams need a multitude of media choices to ensure their communication needs are met.

What are areas of interest for each identified audience segment?

_____

_____

Prepare a Communication Content Strategy

Key Tips:

- ☐ Courtesy is all-important.
- ☐ Tone is also vital.
- ☐ Humor does not travel well.
- ☐ Slow down a little if English is not the first language.
- ☐ Pause and recap fairly frequently when giving a presentation or a speech.
- ☐ Simplify what you have to say and reduce the number of messages and topics.
- ☐ Restate any important statements stressing the word 'not' more than once (people mentally edit this out).
- ☐ Coach senior managers going overseas to give speeches to engage in simple pleasantries in the language of the country. Even if they then resort back to English for the main part of their talk it at least shows they have been prepared to make an effort.

☐ Share best practice across locations.

Content idea: **Content formats** **

** (video, written posts (digital), blogs, articles, guides, ebooks, brochures, magazines (print), images, live streams, infographics, announcements, contests, testimonials, reviews, templates)

_____   _____

_____   _____

_____   _____

_____   _____

_____   _____

_____   _____

_____   _____

Organizational Communication Categories:

Day to Day Communication
☐ organization news;
☐ awards, etc;
☐ housekeeping – pay, appraisals, appointments, operational, etc;
☐ interpreting external media coverage;
☐ listening and responding to worries, etc.

Change Communication
☐ explaining vision, purpose and values;
☐ helping leaders talk with their teams;
☐ sharing knowledge and best practice;
☐ embedding change initiatives;
☐ listening for reactions;
☐ understanding responses to change;
☐ celebrating team success;
☐ industry and other 'bigger picture' news.

Marketing Communication
☐ creating passion about product;
☐ internal marketing activity;
☐ inviting critique and discussion;
☐ marketing programs;
☐ visual environment (buildings etc).

* See Appendix A for additional types of internal communications

Sample Subjects of Interest to Employees:

- ☐ Organizational plans for the future;
- ☐ Job advancement opportunities;
- ☐ Job-related how-to information
- ☐ Productivity improvements;
- ☐ Personnel policies and practices;
- ☐ How we're doing vs the competition;
- ☐ How my job fits into the organization;
- ☐ How external events affect job;
- ☐ How profits are used;
- ☐ Financial results;

Create and send out an employee survey to identify communication gaps. *(*See Appendix B for sample questions to assist you in developing your survey.)*

Create a content calendar.

For each content idea complete the following:

Content Idea: _____

_____

_____

_____

Publication Platform:

☐ *Events:* ☐ Speaking Engagement ☐ Live Streams ☐ Webinar ☐ Podcast

☐ *Social Media:* ☐ YouTube ☐ LinkedIn ☐ Instagram ☐ X (formerly Twitter) ☐ Facebook ☐ ____

___

☐ *Print:* ☐ Newsletter ☐ White Papers ☐ Magazine

☐ *Public Relation:* ☐ Press Release ☐ Announcement ☐ Outreach ☐ Speech

☐ *Other:* _____

Type: ☐ Video ☐ Carousel ☐ Feed Post

☐ Story/Short ☐ Article ☐ Podcast

Publication (Live) Date: _____

Internal Due Date: _____

Assignee: _____

Place Due Date & Live Date onto your calendar:

—Sample Month—

SUNDAY	MONDAY	TUESDAY	WEDNESDAY	THURSDAY	FRIDAY	SATURDAY
		1 Social Media Post	*2* Blog Post Due	*3* Social Media Post	*4*	*5*
6	*7* Social Media Post	*8* State of the Company Live Stream	*9* Social Media Post	*10*	*11* Social Media Post Blog Post Due	*12*
13	*14* Blog Post Due	*15* Social Media Post	*16*	*17* Social Media Post	*18* Employee Newsletter	*19*
20	*21* Social Media Post	*22* State of the Company Live Stream	*23* Social Media Post	*24* Blog Post Due	*25* Social Media Post	*26*
27	*28*	*29* Social Media Post Blog Post Due	*30*	*31* Social Media Post		

See APPENDIX C: Monthly Content Calendar

As you can see for the sample monthly calendar above each piece of content will be planned, developed and rolled out in a consistent and sequential manner. Some of the content may be for both internal and external audiences (like the social media posts) but there will be other pieces that are strictly for internal. Keep in mind that all content that is presented to external audiences needs to be consistent with the internal messaging. You also need to ensure that you employees know about any externally promoted events so that they are in a position to support and fulfill any client questions or requests made about the event.

Create Specific Campaigns

Step 1: Determine Your Objective and Budget. Here are three ways for deciding on your budget.

A. Set your budget by task:

Task/Objective   Budget

_____   _____

_____   _____

_____   _____

_____   _____

B. Match your competitor's budget, by estimate

C. Percentage of sales *(Can range anywhere from 2-20 percent of projected sales)*

Step 2: Identify Your Target Audience

See section C - Assess your Audience

Step 3: Create Your Message

A. TOPIC: _____

B. Appeal to your audience's emotions to evoke an emotional response. _____

_____

_____

C. How does your product or service solve their problem, and/or benefit them afterwards. _____

_____

_____

D. Provide credibility. _____

_____

_____

Step 4: Develop Your Media Strategy

A. Is this a: ☐ Trend (here to stay) or a ☐ Fad (come and go)

   Channel: ☐ Online Media ☐ Direct Marketing ☐ PR
        ☐ Print *(See Section F)*

B. When should it be published? _____

C. Timeline for deployment of individual assets associated with campaign
  - Match content types by topic and audience
  - Define time frame and frequency
  - Delegate campaign roles within the team

Activity	Date	Channel	Resp. Party
_____	_____	_____	_____
_____	_____	_____	_____
_____	_____	_____	_____
_____	_____	_____	_____
_____	_____	_____	_____
_____	_____	_____	_____

Step 5: Implement Your Marketing Campaign
A. Coordination of scheduling and activities for each part of the campaign

Step 6: Measure and Analyze Your Results *(See Section: Measure Analyze and Improve)*
A. Collect Result and Perform analysis

Determining the Right Channels for Communication

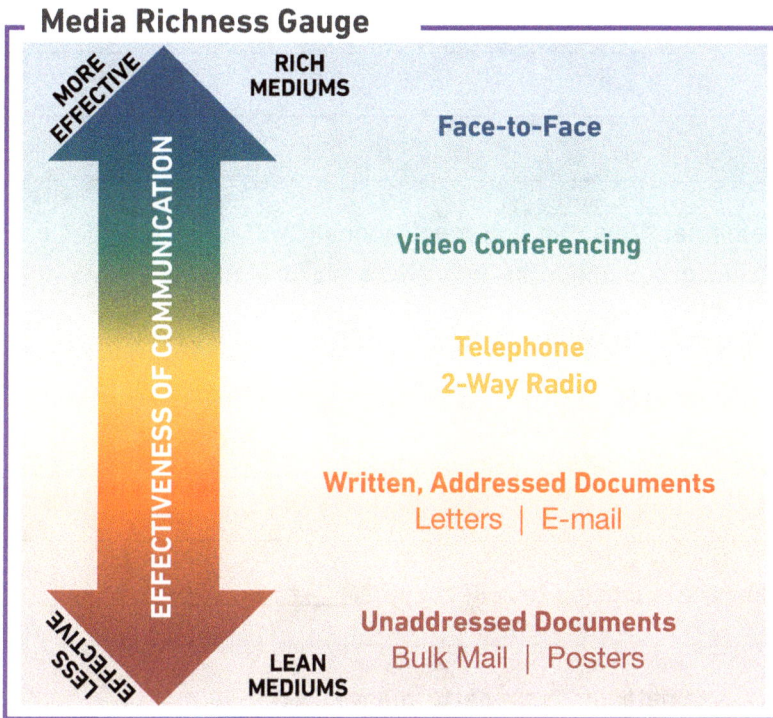

Media Richness Gauge

MORE EFFECTIVE

RICH MEDIUMS

EFFECTIVENESS OF COMMUNICATION

Face-to-Face

Video Conferencing

Telephone
2-Way Radio

Written, Addressed Documents
Letters | E-mail

Unaddressed Documents
Bulk Mail | Posters

LESS EFFECTIVE

LEAN MEDIUMS

Possible communication channels:

- ☐ Face-to-Face/One-on-One
- ☐ Face-to-Face/En Mass
- ☐ Print
- ☐ Broadcast & Audio-Visual
- ☐ Internet Driven
- ☐ Corporate Glue - Games, etc.
- ☐ Events
- ☐ Environment
- ☐ Corporate Social Responsibility

Choose the best channel according to the type and importance ____

_____

_____

_____

Match channels according to target audience and activity_____

_____

_____

_____

Computer-Mediated Communications (CMC) - This includes e-mail, intranet, group networks, websites and social media.

Measure, Analyze, Improve

Collect and centralize data in a repository or tool

What type of data do you want to collect? _____

_____

How are you going to collect data?_____
_____

Analyze data and team performance

Data analysis can be include anything from low-tech paper surveys to comprehensive digital algorithms that track interactions, website page hot spots and bounce rates.

Once you have determined the type of data that you want to collect you will need to develop a system for collection and evaluating if you are meeting established performance goals. This type of data collection and analysis will assist your organization in staying on track both internally and externally with your communication efforts and branding.

What weak spots can you identify that need improvement? _____

_____

_____

_____

Create a detailed report to share reports with everyone in the organization. Sharing your accomplishments helps employees understand the impact of communications and encourages investment.

By creating a regular reporting process to share the success or failure of your marketing campaigns you can improve employee engagement and participation, especially if you provide a positive environment for feedback and suggestions.

These reports should not be dry and boring, but colorful and engaging. Utilizing elements such or branded infographics to help convey messages simply and easily to a broad and diverse audience. Statistically it has been shown that by providing a visual display of information increases retention from 1(hearing) or 2 (reading) to 8 out of 10.

Identify what type of information that you want to share with your internal audience: _____

_____

_____

_____

What would be the best way to share this information? _____

_____

_____

_____

Infographics

When developing infographics there are 5 elements that need to be taken into considerations to ensure that you are creating accessible, memorable, and branded infographics.

1. Type and Layout

There are a variety of types of infographics. What type would be the best for your content?

☐ Statistical   ☐ Informational   ☐ Timeline   ☐ Comparison

What would be the best type of visual layout to present your data?

☐ Graphs   ☐ Flow Charts   ☐ Timeline   ☐ Icons   ☐ Lists

2. Content Narrative

The Infographic needs to connect different pieces of information to tell your audience a story.

☐ Can the reader navigate through the various sections through a seamless narrative flow?

☐ If the information does not support or add to your story - do not include it.

3. Visuals

Do the graphics that you have selected support the story that you want to tell?

☐ Make sure that you are leaving enough white space that all of the elements have room to breath

☐ Try to balance the amount of words images.

4. Words

☐ Keep copy to minimum
☐ Include keywords
☐ Do you have a strong Call to Action?
☐ Do you have an enticing title?
☐ Establish a textual hierarchy

5. Brand Consistency

☐ Use you brand color schemes
☐ Use you brand typefaces
☐ Does your infographic flow seamlessly with your other branded materials?
☐ Simply placing your logo on an infographic is NOT sufficient, it needs to be a true reflection of your brand and provide a consistent experience.

Employee Onboarding

Culture and Policy Training should...

1. Establish what the company stands for and against

2. Outlines expectations for employee behavior

3. Provides HR the opportunity to showcase the "human" side of the organization

When developing your culture and policy training

1. Define your company culture
   - communicate in way that employees can understand
   - tie actions clearly back to the employees job
   - clearly define expectations and how they align with mission, vision & values

2. Provide positive and constructive feedback (employees & management)
   - recognize when employees are doing things right
   - recognize when employees actions support desired culture
   - provide constructive feedback when employee actions do NOT support desired culture
   - empower employees to provide this type of feedback to each other & management

3. Share examples/stories of desired workplace culture
   - highlight examples of desired workplace culture in internal communications (dept meetings, town hall meetings, newsletter, events, etc.)

4. Take swift action
   - if/when their is NOT good culture fit, and redirection & constructive feedback has been unsuccessful, exiting the employee may be necessary to protect the internal culture

5. Monitor & measure
   - Measure the effectiveness of impact on culture

- Simple surveys may be all that is needed

e.g.   • Do employees agree that the desired culture is a
         reality?
        • Do they believe the culture is aligned with the
          organization's mission, vision, and Values?
        • Do they believe they have the tools and resources
          to support that culture?
        • Do they believe the culture contributes to the
          company's success?

Now that we've briefly established the purpose of, and what should be included within your employee onboarding culture and policy training, lets go through the pieces step-by-step to create an onboarding document for your employees. Don't forget that a written document is not the only way this topic can be covered. A video can also be used to show a new employee that your organization is made up of real people and a bit of the culture that they are now stepping into.

Company Mission: _____

_____

_____

_____

Company Values:_____

_____

_____

_____

Our Employees Have VALUE

V - Versatile - _____

_____

A - Authentic - _____

_____

L - Lighthearted - _____

_____

U - Unusual - _____

_____

E - Enthusiastic - _____

_____

Founder(s): _____

_____

Team Leader(s): _____

_____

_____

Policies: _____

_____

_____

_____

_____

Employee Development: _____

_____

_____

_____

_____

Employee Wellness: _____

_____

_____

_____

_____

_____

Culture Examples/Stories: _____

_____

_____

_____

_____

_____

Culture Recognition Program/Policy:_____

_____

_____

_____

_____

_____

_____

Job Description -> Desired Actions: _____

_____

_____

_____

_____

_____

Your company on-boarding documents also serves as a great place to include information about the history of the company, the company organizational structure, future vision and any other branding foundational information that has been developed in the preceding chapters.

I am also a firm believer in the development of your brand persona. For this, you will utilize the elements you developed regarding your Organizational Personality and Voice (see pages 97-99). Here you will use that information to create a "Person" - give them a name - that will embody your organization. This provides a benchmark that your employees can measure against. You want to create a comprehensive person that you and your employees can relate to. Once you have created your persona, then use them regularly to explain and embody the qualities of your brand.

"What would _____ do?" Would be the perfect questions for employees to ask when they are unsure of an action, look, or engagement.

_____

_____

_____

_____

_____

_____

_____

CHAPTER 21

COMPANY CULTURE

Let's break down the concept of company culture. It is the collective set of beliefs, values, norms, behaviors, and practices that shape the identity and character of a specific organization. It includes the "way things are done" or the shared understanding of how things operate within the company. It influences employee interactions. It guides how, where, and when work is done and the overall functioning of the organization. The individual application of elements can, and typically will vary from organization to organization, however the elements themselves are consistent across them all.

Some of the elements of culture will be very familiar to you by this point, but we will review each of them again in context of culture. These consist of core values; vision and purpose; leadership styles; employee engagement; communication and collaboration; employee development and growth; diversity, equity and inclusion; work-life balance; behaviors; and recognition.

The Elements of Culture:

Core Values:

Core values are much more than just words written on a company's website or hung on a plaque in the office. They form the bedrock of an organization's identity and shape its unique culture. These values are the fundamental beliefs and principles that guide the actions, decisions, and everyday behavior of everyone within the organization.

Embedded within the core values is the essence of what the organization stands for and strives to achieve. They act as a compass, providing direction and clarity in times of decision-making, both big and small. The core values serve as a reminder of the organization's mission, vision, and purpose, acting as a guiding force for shaping the company's trajectory.

When core values are thoughtfully defined and effectively

communicated by leadership, they become a powerful force that permeates throughout the entire organization. They help shape the mindset and behavior of employees, fostering a shared sense of purpose and a common understanding of what is truly important. Core values create a cohesive and unified culture, where each individual understands how they contribute to the overall mission and aligns their actions accordingly.

These values can manifest in various ways within the organization. From the way employees interact with one another, to the manner in which they engage with clients and stakeholders, core values influence and shape every aspect of the organization's operations. They act as a guiding compass, ensuring that every individual, regardless of their role, adheres to the same set of principles and beliefs.

Ultimately, core values are the driving force that propels an organization forward. When embraced and lived out by every member of the organization, they create a strong, positive, and purpose-driven company culture that not only attracts and retains top talent but also fosters long-term success and meaningful impact.

What do feel are your practices core values?

_____

_____

Vision and Purpose:

The vision and purpose of an organization go hand in hand in defining its ultimate direction and reason for being. The vision serves as a compelling image of the organization's desired future state. It encapsulates the long-term goals, aspirations, and the impact the organization aims to make in the world. It sets a clear direction and serves as a North Star, guiding the actions and decisions of individuals within the organization.

A well-crafted vision paints a vivid picture of what success looks like, capturing the imagination and inspiring employees to strive towards its realization. It acts as a unifying force, rallying the team around a shared purpose and motivating them to work together towards a common goal. Every employee understands that their individual contributions are vital in achieving the organization's vision.

The purpose of an organization, on the other hand, is deeply rooted in its reason for existence. It answers the question of "why" the organization exists and what societal problem it seeks to solve or what need it aims to fulfill. Purpose brings meaning and fulfillment to employees, as it provides a sense of value and impact in their work.

When an organization's purpose is clearly defined and communicated, it creates a sense of identity and belonging among the employees. They understand that their work goes beyond just completing tasks; they are part of something larger than themselves, making a positive difference in the world.

A well-defined vision and purpose also contribute to fostering a positive company culture. They provide a sense of direction and focus, leading to increased employee engagement, motivation, and satisfaction. When employees understand how their work directly contributes to the organization's overall mission, they feel a greater sense of fulfillment and are more likely to go above and beyond in their roles.

Furthermore, a strong vision and purpose attract like-minded individuals who resonate with the organization's mission. This can lead to a more cohesive and aligned workforce that shares common values and works together towards achieving the organization's goals.

At this point your vision and purpose should be second nature. so I am not going to ask you to write them down here. But, I am going ask - Have you shared the practices' vision and purpose in such a way that your staff not only know the words but have embraced the emotion behind it?

Leadership Style:

The leadership style within an organization has a profound influence on its overall culture. Leaders set the tone and create the environment in which employees work, collaborate, and grow. Their behavior, communication, and decision-making deeply impact the engagement, satisfaction, and well-being of their teams.

Effective leaders recognize the importance of promoting transparency, trust, and inclusivity within the organization. They foster an open and honest environment where information is shared openly, and individuals are encouraged to express their ideas, concerns, and feedback freely. This promotes a culture of transparency, where employees feel valued and empowered, contributing to a positive and collaborative atmosphere.

Trust is another vital element nurtured by effective leadership. Trust is built through consistent integrity, reliability, and accountability. Leaders who trust their employees by delegating responsibilities and providing autonomy foster a sense of ownership and commitment among their teams. Such leaders understand the importance of cultivating an environment where individuals feel safe to take risks, learn from mistakes, and innovate.

Inclusive leadership is also instrumental in shaping a positive company culture. Leaders who embrace diversity and actively seek out different perspectives and opinions create a culture of belonging. They foster an environment where everyone feels respected and valued for their unique contributions. Inclusive leaders encourage collaboration and ensure that diverse voices are heard, leading to better decision-making and creative problem-solving.

On the other hand, poor leadership can have detrimental effects on company culture. Leaders who are authoritarian, micromanaging, or who lack transparency erode trust and hinder collaboration. This can lead to disengagement, low morale, and even high turnover rates within the organization.

Leaders have the power to inspire and motivate their teams. Effective leadership involves clear and consistent communication, providing guidance, setting expectations, and offering support when needed. When leaders communicate with empathy, actively listen to their employees' concerns, and provide timely feedback, they foster a culture of open dialogue and continuous improvement.

Ultimately, leadership style directly influences the overall culture of an organization. The behaviors, actions, and decisions of leaders set the precedent and shape how employees interact, collaborate, and experience their work environment. By emphasizing transparency, trust, inclusivity, and effective communication, leaders can cultivate a positive company culture that promotes employee engagement, satisfaction, and success.

In what ways do you or your leadership team promote transparency?_____

_____ trust?_____

_____ inclusivity?_____

_____

Employee Engagement

Employee engagement is a crucial aspect of a positive company culture. It pertains to the level of involvement, commitment, and motivation displayed by employees towards their work and the overall success of the organization. When employees are engaged, they feel a strong connection to their roles, are invested in the organization's mission, and actively contribute their best efforts.

A culture that encourages and fosters employee engagement creates a work environment where individuals feel valued, supported, and recognized for their contributions. Engaged employees are motivated to go above and beyond their job descriptions, take initiative, and actively seek opportunities for growth and development.

One key factor in fostering employee engagement is recognition.

Appreciating and acknowledging employees' efforts, achievements, and contributions helps create a culture of positive reinforcement. When employees feel valued and appreciated, it boosts their morale and enhances their sense of belonging and loyalty to the organization.

Empowerment is another important element for employee engagement. When employees are given autonomy, trust, and decision-making authority within their roles, they feel empowered and take ownership of their work. This sense of empowerment leads to increased job satisfaction, creativity, and innovation.

Clear communication is fundamental to engage employees in the organization's goals, vision, and strategy. Open channels of communication allow for the exchange of ideas, feedback, and information, creating a culture of transparency and inclusivity. Employees who feel connected and well-informed about the organization's direction are more likely to be engaged and motivated to contribute towards its success.

Additionally, providing opportunities for growth and development is crucial for employee engagement. Organizations that invest in the professional and personal development of their employees demonstrate a commitment to their growth. Offering training programs, learning resources, mentorship opportunities, and career advancement prospects help employees feel supported and motivated to excel in their roles.

Lastly, a work-life balance and a supportive work environment contribute to employee engagement. When employees feel that their well-being is valued, that their work is recognized, and that there is flexibility to manage personal responsibilities, they are more likely to be engaged and motivated to perform at their best.

In what ways does your organization foster employee engagement?

_____

_____

Communication and Collaboration

Communication and collaboration are integral components of a positive company culture. When an organization prioritizes open and transparent communication, it creates an environment where employees feel connected, valued, and engaged. Effective communication channels and feedback mechanisms facilitate the exchange of ideas, information sharing, and active participation, fostering a culture of trust, respect, and inclusivity.

First and foremost, open communication channels enable employees to express their thoughts, ideas, and concerns freely. It creates a sense of psychological safety, where individuals feel comfortable speaking up and sharing their perspectives. This encourages healthy dialogue, innovation, and problem-solving. When employees know that their voices are heard and that their opinions matter, they become more invested in their work, leading to increased satisfaction and engagement.

In addition, organizations that value open communication provide regular updates and share information about key decisions, developments, and company milestones. Transparent communication helps employees understand the organization's vision, mission, and goals, fostering a sense of purpose and alignment. When employees have a clear understanding of the bigger picture and how their work contributes to it, they feel a stronger sense of meaning and ownership, leading to increased motivation and productivity.

Feedback mechanisms are critical in promoting a culture of continuous improvement and growth. Regular and constructive feedback allows employees to learn, course-correct, and develop professionally. When feedback is provided in a timely and respectful manner, it strengthens relationships, enhances performance, and helps individuals reach their full potential. It also fosters trust and collaboration between employees and their supervisors or colleagues.

Collaboration is another vital aspect of a positive company culture. Encouraging teamwork and cross-functional collaboration creates an environment where diverse perspectives are valued, and collective intelligence thrives. Collaboration breaks down silos, encourages knowledge sharing, and enables the generation of innovative solutions. When individuals collaborate effectively, they leverage each other's strengths, leading to higher-quality work outcomes and a sense of collective success.

In what ways are you allowing for open feedback from your employees? How are you encouraging collaboration and open communication? _____

_____

_____

Employee Development and Growth:

Employee development and growth are crucial aspects of a positive company culture. When an organization values and invests in the professional and personal development of its employees, it demonstrates a commitment to their growth and success. Such a culture creates an environment where employees feel supported, motivated, and empowered to enhance their skills, expand their knowledge, and advance in their careers.

Providing training and development opportunities is an effective way to nurture talent within the organization. Offering workshops, seminars, conferences, and online courses enables employees to acquire new skills, stay updated with industry trends, and broaden their capabilities. This not only benefits the individual employee but also contributes to the overall growth and success of the organization.

Mentoring programs are another valuable tool for employee development and growth. Pairing employees with experienced mentors allows for knowledge transfer, guidance, and support. Mentoring relationships provide a platform for employees to develop new perspectives, gain insights, and receive valuable career advice. This fosters a sense of belonging, as employees feel supported and encouraged by more experienced colleagues.

In addition to training and mentoring, providing growth opportunities within the organization is key. Creating clear career paths, internal promotion opportunities, and the chance to take on new responsibilities allow employees to advance in their careers. By recognizing and rewarding employees' efforts and achievements, organizations motivate and retain top talent. Employees who see a future within the organization are more likely to be engaged, committed, and motivated to excel in their roles.

A culture that values employee development and growth also encourages continuous learning. Employers can empower employees to expand their knowledge and skills through initiatives such as lunch-and-learn sessions, book clubs, and cross-training opportunities. Encouraging a growth mindset where employees embrace new challenges and see failure as an opportunity for growth supports a culture of continuous improvement and innovation.

Furthermore, when employees see that their organization invests in their development, it fosters a sense of loyalty and commitment. They perceive that their work is valued, which improves morale and job satisfaction. This positive work environment promotes collaboration, knowledge sharing, and collective growth within the organization.

Is employee development and growth a priority in your practice? If so, how is this implemented?_____

_____

_____

Diversity, Equity, and Inclusion:

Embracing diversity, equity, and inclusion (DEI) within an organization is essential for cultivating a positive company culture. DEI encompasses valuing and embracing the differences and unique perspectives of individuals, promoting fairness, and fostering an inclusive work environment where all employees feel valued and respected.

First and foremost, promoting diversity within the organization goes beyond just representation but aims to create a culture that welcomes individuals from various backgrounds, experiences, and identities. This includes ensuring that hiring practices are inclusive and non-discriminatory, actively seeking out diverse talent, and creating a workplace that reflects the broader communities in which the organization operates. By embracing diversity, organizations can tap into a wider range of ideas, perspectives, and insights, which contributes to innovation and creativity.

Equity is also a crucial pillar of a positive organizational culture. It involves creating fair and just opportunities for all individuals within the workplace. This means providing equal access to resources, benefits, and growth opportunities, regardless of factors such as gender, race, age, or background. A commitment to equity ensures that employees are treated fairly, empowering them to reach their full potential and contribute effectively to the organization's success.

Inclusivity is vital for creating a positive company culture. An inclusive work environment acknowledges and respects the unique contributions and perspectives of every individual. It ensures that everyone feels valued, heard, and empowered to fully participate and thrive within the organization. Inclusive organizations promote open communication, actively seek input from all employees, and provide a safe and supportive space for diverse voices to be heard.

To foster a culture of diversity, equity, and inclusion, organizations can implement various initiatives. This includes offering diversity and inclusion training for employees to raise awareness, providing cultural competency programs to enhance understanding, and establishing Employee Resource Groups (ERGs) to offer support and networking opportunities for underrepresented groups. It is also crucial for leaders to demonstrate a commitment to DEI by modeling inclusive behaviors and consistently reinforcing the organization's values.

A positive company culture that embraces DEI has numerous benefits. It improves employee morale, engagement, and satisfaction, as individuals feel valued and included. Embracing diversity fosters innovation and creativity, as different perspectives lead to more robust problem-solving and decision-making. Additionally, organizations that prioritize diversity and inclusion are more attractive to top talent, leading to a more diverse and talented workforce.

What steps has your practice taken to foster a culture of diversity, equity, and inclusion? _____

_____

_____

Work-Life Balance:

Work-life balance is a crucial aspect of a positive company culture. It refers to the equilibrium between professional responsibilities and personal well-being that allows employees to effectively manage their work commitments while also addressing their personal and family needs.

A company culture that prioritizes work-life balance demonstrates a commitment to the well-being of its employees. By providing flexible work options, such as remote work or flexible hours, organizations empower employees to have more control over their schedules. This flexibility allows individuals to better manage their personal responsibilities, whether it's caring for family members, pursuing personal hobbies, or maintaining a healthy lifestyle.

Promoting work-life integration is another important element of fostering a positive company culture. Work-life integration allows employees to seamlessly blend their personal and professional lives, rather than viewing them as separate and conflicting domains. By encouraging a healthy integration, organizations acknowledge that employees have commitments and interests outside of work. This can involve supporting employees' involvement in their communities, offering resources or programs for achieving work-life harmony, and implementing policies that encourage employees to take time off for personal well-being.

Recognizing the importance of employee well-being is vital in creating a positive work environment. Encouraging employees to prioritize self-care, recharge, and maintain a healthy work-life balance fosters a culture that values and supports their physical, mental, and emotional health. This can be done through wellness programs, providing access to resources for stress management or mental health support, and promoting a healthy work environment that values breaks, rest, and relaxation.

Organizations that prioritize work-life balance also benefit in multiple ways. Employees with a healthy work-life balance tend to be more engaged, motivated, and productive. They experience reduced stress levels and have higher job satisfaction, leading to improved retention rates. Additionally, a positive work-life balance can enhance the organization's reputation and attractiveness to top talent, as individuals seek workplaces that prioritize employee well-being.

Does your practice have any policies or initiatives in place that support your employees with balancing commitments of both their personal and work lives? What about self-care? _____

_____

_____

Interplay of elements

Now that we have gone over the some of the main element of culture it's time to look at how they interact with each other and how they work together to create the culture in your practice.

Behaviors:

Company culture behaviors refer to the actions, attitudes, and values that are demonstrated and practiced by employees within a particular organization. Company culture encompasses the shared beliefs, norms, and practices *(these come from the core values, vision and purpose and are shaped by the leadership style)* that shape the behavior of employees and influence how they interact with one another, make decisions, and approach their work. Here are some examples of company culture behaviors:

1.   **Collaboration:** Employees in a company with a collaborative culture work together, share ideas, and support each other in achieving common goals. Collaboration is encouraged and valued, and employees actively seek out opportunities to work cross-functionally and share knowledge and expertise.

2.   **Respect:** Respectful behavior is a key aspect of a positive company culture. Employees treat each other with respect, regardless of their role or level in the organization. This includes showing consideration for diversity and inclusion, and valuing different perspectives and opinions.

3.   **Innovation:** A culture that encourages innovation fosters creativity, experimentation, and continuous improvement. Employees are encouraged to come up with new ideas, share them openly, and are provided with resources and support to pursue innovative solutions to challenges.

4.   **Accountability:** A culture of accountability promotes ownership and responsibility for one's work and actions. Employees take ownership of their tasks, meet deadlines, and are willing to take responsibility for their mistakes and learn from them.

5.   **Ethical behavior:** Ethical behavior is emphasized in a positive company culture. Employees are expected to act with integrity, follow company policies and procedures, and adhere to legal and ethical standards in all aspects of their work.

6.   **Communication:** Effective communication is a fundamental element of a healthy company culture. Employees communicate openly, transparently, and respectfully with their colleagues and managers. Feedback is given and received constructively, and communication channels are encouraged to be open and accessible.

7.   **Work-life balance:** A company culture that values work-life balance acknowledges the importance of personal well-being and

encourages employees to maintain a healthy balance between work and personal life. This includes offering flexibility in working hours, providing support for work-life integration, and promoting a healthy work-life balance.

8. **Continuous learning:** A culture of continuous learning emphasizes the importance of professional development and growth. Employees are encouraged to acquire new skills, pursue training and development opportunities, and share knowledge with their peers.

9. **Customer focus:** A patient-centric culture places a strong emphasis on understanding and meeting the needs of patients. Employees are encouraged to prioritize patient satisfaction, actively listen to patient feedback, and take appropriate actions to deliver excellent patient service.

These are just some examples of company culture behaviors, and different organizations may have their own unique set of behaviors that align with their values, vision, and mission. A positive company culture with desirable behaviors can contribute to higher employee engagement, increased productivity, improved teamwork, and a healthier work environment, leading to overall organizational success.

Take a moment and think about what behaviors currently exist within your practice. Are these the behaviors that you want to reflect your practices culture? If not, what needs to change to precipitate a change in employee behavior? _____

_____

_____

Recognition:

Company culture recognition refers to the acknowledgment and appreciation of a positive company culture within an organization. It involves recognizing and celebrating the behaviors, values, and norms that contribute to a healthy and positive company culture.

Recognizing and acknowledging company culture can have several benefits, including:

1. **Employee engagement:** Recognizing and appreciating the company culture can boost employee engagement. When employees see that their efforts to live out the company's values and behaviors are recognized and appreciated, it can increase their motivation and commitment to the organization.

2. **Retention and loyalty:** Recognizing company culture can help with employee retention and loyalty. Employees who feel valued for their contribution to the company culture are more likely to stay with the organization and be loyal to it over the long term.

3. **Reinforcement of positive behaviors:** Recognizing company culture behaviors reinforces the desired behaviors within the organization. When employees see that their behaviors are recognized and rewarded, they are more likely to continue exhibiting those behaviors, contributing to the sustainability of the company culture.

4. **Positive impact on performance:** Recognizing and appreciating company culture can positively impact employee performance. It can create a sense of pride and ownership among employees, leading to higher levels of productivity, collaboration, and innovation.

5. **Enhanced organizational reputation:** A positive company culture can enhance the overall reputation of the organization. When the company's culture and values are recognized and appreciated, it can contribute to a positive perception among patients, partners, and other stakeholders, enhancing the organization's reputation in the market.

Company culture recognition can be done through various means, such as regular communication, rewards and recognition programs, appreciation events, internal newsletters, social media, and other channels that align with the organization's values and communication style. It's important to ensure that the recognition efforts are *genuine*, consistent, and aligned with the company's culture and values to have a meaningful impact on employee morale, engagement, and overall organizational success.

Does your practice have employee recognition programs in place? If so, are they well received by your staff? If not, what could you put in place that would recognize positive cultural contributions? _____

_____

_____

_____

Rituals:

Company culture rituals are regular and recurring activities, events, or practices within an organization that are designed to reinforce and promote the company's values, behaviors, and overall culture. These rituals serve as symbolic actions that help employees connect with the organization's culture, build relationships, and create a sense of community and belonging. Some examples of company culture rituals include:

1.   **Onboarding rituals:** These are rituals or activities that are part of the new employee on-boarding process and are designed to help new hires understand and embrace the company's culture. This can include activities like an orientation program, welcome events, culture workshops, and mentorship programs.

2.   **Recognition rituals:** These are rituals that acknowledge and appreciate employees who embody the company's culture and values. This can include regular recognition programs, awards ceremonies, shout-outs in team meetings, and other forms of public recognition for employees who demonstrate the desired behaviors.

3.   **Celebratory rituals:** These are rituals that celebrate milestones, achievements, and successes of the organization and its employees. This can include anniversary celebrations, holiday parties, team-building activities, and other events that bring employees together to celebrate and reinforce the company's culture.

4. **Communication rituals:** These are rituals that facilitate open and transparent communication within the organization, promoting a culture of trust and collaboration. This can include regular town hall meetings, team huddles, employee surveys, and feedback sessions, where employees are encouraged to share their thoughts, ideas, and concerns.

5. **Social rituals:** These are informal and social activities that foster relationships, team bonding, and a sense of community among employees. This can include casual gatherings, team lunches, after-work events, and other social activities that provide opportunities for employees to connect with each other and build relationships beyond work tasks.

6. **Wellness rituals:** These are rituals that promote employee well-being and a healthy work-life balance, which are integral parts of many company cultures today. This can include wellness programs, fitness challenges, mindfulness sessions, and other activities that prioritize the physical and mental well-being of employees.

Company culture rituals should be aligned with the organization's values, purpose, and overall culture. They should be inclusive, engaging, and relevant to the employees to have a meaningful impact on reinforcing the desired culture and fostering a positive work environment.

What rituals does your practice currently have in place? _____

_____

_____

_____

Cues:

Company culture cues are the tangible and intangible elements within an organization that reflect and influence the company's culture. These cues can be observed in various aspects of the work environment, communication, behaviors, and practices of employees, leadership styles, and organizational policies. Company culture cues can include:

1.   **Physical environment:** The physical layout, design, and decor of the workplace can convey important cues about the company culture. For example, an open office layout with collaborative spaces and common areas may reflect a culture that values teamwork and innovation, while a more traditional office setup with closed doors and hierarchical spaces may reflect a more formal and hierarchical culture.

2.   **Artifacts and symbols:** Artifacts and symbols such as the company logo, mission statement, core values, and other visual elements used in the workplace can convey important cues about the company culture. These elements are often displayed on walls, signage, websites, and other communication materials, and they serve as visual cues that reinforce the company's cultural identity.

3.   **Language and communication:** The language and communication style used within the organization can also be a cue to the company culture. This includes the use of specific terms, jargon, and tone of communication, as well as the frequency and channels of communication. For example, a company culture that values transparency and inclusivity may have open and frequent communication across all levels of the organization.

4.   **Behaviors and practices:** The behaviors and practices of employees and leaders within the organization can be strong cues to the company culture. This includes how employees interact with each other, how decisions are made, how conflicts are resolved, and how performance is recognized and rewarded. For example, a company culture that values collaboration and empowerment may encourage open discussions, employee involvement in decision-making, and recognition of team efforts.

5.   **Leadership styles:** The leadership styles and behaviors of leaders within the organization can also influence the company culture. Leaders serve as role models and set the tone for the organization's

culture through their actions and behaviors. For example, a leadership style that is inclusive, transparent, and empowers employees may foster a culture of trust, collaboration, and innovation.

6. **Policies and practices:** The organizational policies, practices, and procedures also play a role in shaping the company culture cues. This includes policies related to diversity and inclusion, performance management, employee benefits, and other practices that reflect the organization's values and priorities.

It's important to note that company culture cues can be both explicit and implicit, and they may be consciously designed or may emerge organically. They collectively contribute to the overall perception and experience of the company culture by employees, patients, partners, and other stakeholders. Therefore, it's crucial for organizations to be intentional about shaping their culture cues to align with their desired culture and values.

These are some of the key elements that make up company culture. It's important to note that company culture is unique to each organization and may evolve over time. A positive company culture can contribute to employee satisfaction, engagement, productivity, and overall organizational success.

Describe the cultural cues that exist in your practice. Do these reflect the type of culture that you want? If not, how can you change it? _____

_____

_____

_____

_____

_____

_____

Changing Culture

Changing your culture isn't easy. A band-aid patch on any one issue isn't going to do it. Culture can only be changed from the top down. What this means is that if LEADERSHIP doesn't buy in then forget anyone else doing so.

Culture is just like every other piece in the branding puzzle. It starts at the top. It must be bought into and lived at the top of the organization, and at every step down in order for it to be *authentic* and for your staff to *feel* the truth in what is being said. You don't want your branding to be just words, and your company culture CAN'T be just words. To be honest your culture is your brand,- and your brand is your culture because how your people treat patients, and each other in front of the patients, will become your brand. One of my favorite statements is that **your least paid employee is most often your front line brand ambassador.** Think about that for a moment.

Who is your least paid employee? What do they do? Do they interact directly with your patients? Are they *happy*? If they're not, what are your patients getting? What are *prospects* getting?

This isn't a call to pay them more... it's about culture. Are they recognized? Are they appreciated? Are they listened to? Are their concerns viewed as valid? Do they have a way of even voicing their concerns? Although, technically "not your problem", are they having problems away from work? Do they need support in their personal lives? Is their a way they can reach out for support if they need it? As you've read through this chapter you've touched on many topics that would create support for this hypothetical employee.

Maybe you have a wellness program that offers talk therapy, maybe you have a work-life program that allows for flexible scheduling so they can pick up their child from school because they won't ride the bus. Maybe its a recognition program that acknowledges they do a good job and are seen.

These actions can take someone whose nearly broken and give

them a spark to *want* to get up and come to work in the morning. A joy to speak up for *their* company, because their company cares about them. You will never find a better brand ambassador, and you may never know.

Okay, so how to get there.

Hopefully, you've gone through and evaluated your practice at each stage throughout this chapter. Now we need to look at those evaluations and create a plan of action. Go back through your answers and any where you noted that you needed to change, add, or create a program write it down.

_____

_____

_____

_____

_____

_____

_____

_____

_____

What programs are going to best serve your practice and be in alignment with your brand and the culture you want to create?

_____

_____

_____

_____

_____

How will you get Leadership buy in (if it's just you it's easy)? How will you convince partners/managers of its importance? _____

_____

_____

_____

_____

How will you communicate the new programs to staff? You need their buy in and participation as well. (Remember OPEN communication, be willing to hear & accept their feedback.)_____

_____

_____

_____

_____

It will take time. Like all behavioral changes, they don't happen overnight, but they do happen. But, you are now on your way to the internal culture you want. Remember to recognize the positives, reprimand the negative behaviors and if their is nonconformity you may have to let someone go in order to let the practice culture shift. Unfortunately, not everyone is willing to change, and sometime that means you have to separate for the benefit of everyone else. It's not ideal, and sometimes painful, but if you want a new culture you must stay focused on the longterm goal and do what is necessary to move the practice in that direction.

PART 5

Social & Reputation

Management

"The best brands are built on great stories."

— Ian Rowden,
former Chief Marketing Officer at Virgin Group

Ian Rowden is a highly accomplished marketing executive who served as the Chief Marketing Officer (CMO) at Virgin Group, a multinational conglomerate known for its diverse portfolio of businesses. As the CMO, Rowden played a vital role in shaping the marketing strategies and brand experiences across various Virgin companies, including Virgin Atlantic, Virgin Hotels, Virgin Mobile, and more. With his deep understanding of the Virgin brand and its core values, Rowden led marketing initiatives that emphasized customer-centricity, innovation, and disruption. His expertise in brand development, digital marketing, and customer experience helped enhance the impact and differentiation of the Virgin brand in highly competitive industries. Throughout his tenure, Rowden contributed significantly to reinforce Virgin's reputation as a dynamic and customer-focused brand, always pushing boundaries and challenging conventional norms.

CHAPTER 22

OUTWARD EXPOSURE

Now that you have created your foundational branding and internal cultural structures, establishing the external supports will come more easily. This chapter focuses on developing the processes and procedures your organization will use to ensure brand standards when engaging with the public, clients, and prospects. These strategies are designed to help your organization stand out from the competition, reinforce your goals and values, and ensure that you are seen as you wish to be.

What is Outward Exposure?

Let's clarify what is meant by the outward-facing elements of your branding. These are the elements visible to your potential clients, patients, or the general public. They include:

- **Marketing Materials:** Advertisements, direct mails, etc.
- **Press Releases:** News about your practice, awards, or recognitions.
- **TV/Video and Radio Ads:** Media spots that promote your practice.
- **Social Media:** Posts that represent your practice and engage with the audience.
- **Events:** Public relations events that you or your staff participate in.
- **Articles:** Magazine articles or news reports about you or your practice.
- **External Signage:** Signs that identify and promote your practice.
- **Website:** Your online presence that provides information and engages with the public.

Examples of these elements include a magazine article about your practice, staff appearances in the news, events, or awards and recognitions your practice has received. While you don't have total control over every piece of outward exposure, you do have significant influence, especially when it comes to social media. Once a post has gone live, it's "in the wild," but you control the initial post and your responses to any engagement it receives.

Consistency is key in all these elements. Whether it's the tone, visuals, or overall feel of the piece, it should be easily identifiable as coming from your practice.

Importance of Standard Operating Procedures (SOPs) in Relation to Brand Consistency

As we discussed in the beginning of Chapter 4:

Branding refers to the process of creating a unique and recognizable identity for a product, service, company, or individual. It involves developing a distinctive name, logo, tagline, design, and overall visual and verbal representation that sets apart a brand from its competitors and conveys its core values, personality, and promises to its target audience.

Branding is not limited to just a logo or visual elements, but it also encompasses the emotional and psychological connection that consumers have with a brand. It is not just about creating a consistent and cohesive brand experience across all touchpoints, including advertising, marketing materials, packaging, website, social media, patient service, and more.

With this in mind, it makes logical since to put into place standards and guidelines that would help us, our current staff, and any future players (vendors or consultants) that may come along maintain that consistency and integrity of the brand that you have worked diligently to create.

If you have been actively working through this book, then you have most of the information you need to complete these standard operating procedures (SOPs) already in your hands.

Visuals

Visual consistency is an easy and impactful way of creating

cohesion across all of your assets. By utilizing the same color palette, typefaces, and style of imagery, you can easily make all of your visual assets feel as pieces of a collective whole and establish a "look" for your brand.

When it come to establishing SOPs for the visual elements, adherence to your brand standards is at the top of your list. You should also set into place a repository of approved images, so that your team know what to use without worrying about going outside of the visual style specifications. Image selection can be difficult, and if your brand has a very specific style, providing staff with a pre-selected repository eliminates the use of images that do not meet the brand standards.

Depending on the size of your staff, you may want to designate one or more individuals to act as keepers of the brand. These individuals would be responsible for signing off on the brand before anything went out the door. They would look over presentations, marketing materials, vendor/contractor work, to ensure that colors, type, images used, tone of voice, expression, and the emotional impact of each piece all are in adherence to the brand.

Tone and Expression

Every communication you send out should be in sync with your brand's tone. It requires:
- **Setting a Clear Tone:** Whether it's formal, playful, or empathetic.
- **Establishing SOPs:** Procedures to ensure every communication maintains this tone.

Emotional Impact

Brands that resonate emotionally tend to have a stronger recall. Thus, we must:
- **Understand Our Brand's Emotional Quotient:** What feelings do we want to evoke?
- **Set SOPs:** Ensure every branding effort touches the right

emotional chords.

Essential Branding Assets

Introduction to the tools and assets that help in maintaining outward exposure.

Brand Strategy: The blueprint of what we stand for.

A brand strategy document is a structured plan that outlines a company's understanding of its brand identity, its goals in communicating this identity, and the specific tactics it will use to achieve these goals. It is the blueprint for how a brand presents itself to the world, ensuring consistency, clarity, and effective communication at every touchpoint.

COMPONENTS OF A BRAND STRATEGY DOCUMENT:

BRAND OVERVIEW:
- **Mission:** The core purpose of the business. What are its primary goals and objectives?
- **Vision:** Where does the company see itself in the future? What is the long-term aim?
- **Values:** The principles and beliefs that guide the company's actions and decisions.

TARGET AUDIENCE:
- **Demographics:** Age, gender, location, income, and other measurable statistics.
- **Psychographics:** Values, beliefs, interests, lifestyles, and other qualitative attributes.
- **User Personas:** Fictional characters created to represent different user types.

BRAND POSITIONING:
- **Unique Value Proposition (UVP):** What sets the company apart from its competitors?
- **Positioning Statement:** A concise description of the brand's unique value and its target audience.

TONE OF VOICE:

- **Personality:** Is the brand formal, playful, serious, or empathetic?
- **Communication Style:** How does the brand communicate its messages across various channels?

VISUAL IDENTITY:

- **Logo:** Design, variations, and guidelines for usage.
- **Color Palette:** Primary and secondary colors with codes.
- **Typography:** Preferred fonts for headlines, body text, and other content.
- **Imagery:** Guidelines for photos, illustrations, and other visual media.

BRAND MESSAGING:

- **Taglines and Slogans:** Short, catchy phrases that encapsulate the brand's essence.
- **Brand Story:** A narrative that conveys the brand's history, purpose, and values.
- **Key Messages:** Core statements that the brand wants to communicate to its audience.

BRAND TOUCHPOINTS:

- **Physical:** Storefronts, packaging, business cards, etc.
- **Digital:** Website, social media profiles, email campaigns, etc.
- **Human:** Customer service interactions, sales processes, etc.

COMPETITIVE ANALYSIS:

- **Market Landscape:** Overview of the industry and key players.
- **SWOT Analysis:** Strengths, Weaknesses, Opportunities, and Threats of the brand in its current position.

GOALS AND KPIs:

- **Short-term Goals:** Milestones to be achieved in the upcoming months.
- **Long-term Goals:** Aims for the coming years.
- **Key Performance Indicators:** Metrics used to measure the success of the brand strategy.

IMPLEMENTATION AND GUIDELINES:
- **Brand Guidelines:** A separate document or section detailing how the brand elements should be used.
- **Content Strategy:** Plan for content creation and distribution.
- **Engagement Strategy:** How the brand will interact with its audience.

In essence, a brand strategy document serves as a comprehensive guide that ensures all branding efforts by Neurotic Dog Studios align with its core values, goals, and vision. It is both a strategic tool and a reference document that ensures the brand remains consistent and true to its identity across all communications and interactions.

Brand Standards: Details on our visual and tonal guidelines.

Brand standards, also known as brand guidelines or style guides, are a set of rules and specifications that define how a brand is presented and communicated across different mediums. These guidelines provide a consistent framework for businesses, like Neurotic Dog Studios, ensuring that their brand's identity is coherent, consistent, and effectively resonates with the target audience.

COMPONENTS OF BRAND STANDARDS:

LOGO GUIDELINES:
- **Usage:** Define where and how the logo can be used.
- **Size & Placement:** Specify minimum size, scaling rules, and spacing around the logo.
- **Variations:** Outline different versions of the logo (e.g., monochrome, vertical, horizontal) and when each should be used.
- **Misuse:** Illustrate common mistakes to avoid, such as distorting the logo or using it on a clashing background.

COLOR PALETTE:
- **Primary Colors:** Core colors that represent the brand.
- **Secondary Colors:** Supporting colors that complement the primary ones.

- **Tertiary Colors:** Additional colors, if any, used in specific instances.
- **Color Codes:** Provide RGB, CMYK, Pantone, and HEX codes to ensure accurate replication.

TYPOGRAPHY:

- **Primary Typefaces:** Fonts used for headlines or key messaging.
- **Secondary Typefaces:** Fonts used for body text, captions, or other supporting text.
- **Usage Guidelines:** Outline when and where each typeface should be used.

IMAGERY:

- **Photography Style:** Define the mood, composition, and subjects of photos associated with the brand.
- **Illustration Style:** If applicable, guidelines on the style, colors, and usage of illustrations.
- **Iconography:** Define the style and usage of icons associated with the brand.

TONE OF VOICE:

- **Personality:** Describe the brand's character—whether it's professional, friendly, playful, etc.
- **Language & Grammar:** Specify any preferred terms, phrases, or grammar rules.
- **Dos and Don'ts:** Provide examples of how the brand should and shouldn't communicate.

Layout and Design:

- **Grid Systems:** Outline any grids or layout structures preferred for various mediums.
- **Margins and Spacing:** Define the spacing around various elements for consistency.
- **Hierarchy:** Explain the order of importance for design elements.

SETTING UP BRAND STANDARDS:

- **Assess the Brand:** Start with a clear understanding of the brand's mission, vision, values, and target audience.
- **Gather Existing Materials:** Look at all current branding materials and identify what aligns with the brand's vision and what needs modification.
- **Collaborate:** Engage with design, marketing, and other relevant teams to get diverse perspectives. This collaboration will ensure the standards are both comprehensive and practical.
- **Develop the Guidelines:** Based on your assessments and collaboration, start defining each component of the brand standards. Utilize visual examples wherever possible.
- **Test & Refine:** Before finalizing, test the guidelines. Create mock-ups or prototypes to see how the brand standards work in practice. Refine based on these tests.
- **Documentation:** Create a well-organized, easily accessible document (or set of documents). Digital formats, like PDFs, are popular, but online brand portals or printed booklets can also be beneficial.
- **Educate & Distribute:** Ensure everyone within Neurotic Dog Studios is familiar with the brand standards. Provide training sessions if necessary and make the guidelines easily accessible to all team members.
- **Review Periodically:** Brand standards should evolve as the brand grows. Set periodic reviews to ensure they remain relevant and effective.

By setting up clear brand standards, you can ensure that every piece of communication, whether digital or print, internal or external, consistently reflects the brand's essence, ensuring recognition and trustworthiness in the market.

Templates: Pre-designed formats for various purposes, ensuring consistency.

For a practice, especially one focused on health and wellness providers maintaining consistent branding across various touchpoints is crucial. Here are the types of templates a practice should consider having to ensure brand consistency:

STATIONERY TEMPLATES:
- **Letterhead:** A standardized format for official communications.
- **Business Cards:** For employees to share contact details professionally.
- **Envelopes:** Customized envelopes with the practice's branding.

DIGITAL ASSETS:
- **Email Signature:** A consistent footer for all official emails.
- **Email Newsletter:** A standard layout for regular communications to clients or subscribers.
- **PowerPoint/Slide Deck:** For presentations, ensuring they carry the brand's identity.
- **Social Media Graphics:** Templates for posts, stories, banners, and profile images.

MARKETING MATERIALS:
- **Brochures:** Informational print material about the practice's services.
- **Flyers:** For events, promotions, or announcements.
- **Postcards:** Useful for direct mail marketing campaigns.
- **Banners & Posters:** For physical advertising or events.
- **Ads:** Standardized templates for print and digital advertisements.

CLIENT-FACING DOCUMENTS:
- **Appointment Cards:** Reminders for patients about upcoming appointments.
- **Prescription Sheets:** Branded templates for medical prescriptions.
- **Invoice and Billing:** Consistent layouts for financial interactions.
- **Patient Information Forms:** Standardized forms for new patients or updates.

ONLINE PRESENCE:
- **Website Elements:** Banners, footers, and other recurrent website graphics.
- **Webinar Graphics:** For online seminars or informational sessions.
- **Digital Ad Banners:** For online advertising campaigns.

INTERNAL COMMUNICATIONS:
- **Internal Memos:** For intra-office communications.
- **Employee Onboarding Packs:** Materials for new hires to familiarize them with the brand and its values.
- **Report Templates:** For internal reporting and data presentation.

EVENT MATERIALS:
- **Event Invitations:** For seminars, workshops, or other events.
- **Event Signage:** Banners, standees, and booth graphics for events or fairs.
- **Name Tags/Badges:** For employees and attendees during events.

PROMOTIONAL MERCHANDISE:
- **T-shirt Designs:** For events or as merchandise.
- **Tote Bags, Mugs, and Other Merchandise:** Carry the brand for promotional or sale purposes.

GUIDELINE DOCUMENTS:
- **Brand Guidelines:** A reference document detailing the use of logos, colors, typography, etc.
- **Content Guidelines:** For writers and content creators to maintain a consistent brand voice.

VIDEO AND MULTIMEDIA:
- **Video Intros/Outros:** Branded beginnings or conclusions to video content.
- **Podcast Covers:** If the practice engages in podcasting or audio content.

To set up these templates, it's essential to ensure that the design aligns with the brand's guidelines in terms of colors, typography, imagery, and overall style. They should also be easily accessible to team members and reviewed periodically to ensure they stay relevant and updated.

Having these templates in place ensures that every interaction potential clients have with Neurotic Dog Studios conveys a unified and professional image, reinforcing the brand's credibility and trustworthiness.

Additional Tools: Software for brand management and other essential assets.

Software for brand management

Other assets (e.g., media kits, style guides)

Conclusion

Managing outward exposure is paramount for establishing a brand that resonates and leaves an imprint. By using this guide and the subsequent resources, we at Neurotic Dog Studios can ensure that every branding effort is consistent, authentic, and impactful.

Additional Resources

Brand management tools are essential for ensuring that a brand maintains consistency, efficiency, and effectiveness across various touchpoints. Here's a list of tools that can aid in brand management:

BRAND MANAGEMENT SOFTWARE:
- **Adobe Creative Cloud:** Tools like Illustrator (for vector design), Photoshop (for image editing), and InDesign (for layout) are industry standards for creating brand assets.
- **Canva:** A user-friendly design tool with pre-made templates, suitable for creating social media graphics, presentations, and other branded content.
- **Widen Collective:** A Digital Asset Management (DAM) system that centralizes brand assets, making them easily accessible

to team members.

- **Bynder:** Another DAM tool, Bynder also offers brand guidelines portals, creative project management, and automated templates.
- **Frontify:** Provides brand guidelines, asset libraries, and design collaboration in one place.
- **Lucidpress:** A brand templating platform that ensures brand consistency across various materials.
- **Canto:** A DAM solution that focuses on simplifying the organization and retrieval of brand assets.
- **Brandfolder:** Helps businesses centralize and share their brand assets, track usage, and get insights on asset performance.

COLLABORATION & WORKFLOW TOOLS:
- **Trello or Asana:** Project management tools that can be used to track branding projects, campaigns, or initiatives.
- **Slack:** A communication platform that can be used for internal discussions about brand campaigns, designs, and strategies.
- **InVision or Figma:** Tools for design collaboration, prototyping, and feedback collection.

SOCIAL MEDIA MANAGEMENT:
- **Hootsuite or Buffer:** Platforms for scheduling, publishing, and analyzing social media content across multiple channels, ensuring brand consistency.
- **Sprout Social:** Offers social media management, monitoring, and analytics to ensure the brand's voice remains consistent online.

MONITORING & ANALYTICS:
- **Google Analytics:** Provides insights into website traffic, helping to understand how the brand performs online.
- **Brandwatch:** A tool for monitoring brand mentions across the internet, providing insights into brand perception.
- **SEMrush or Ahrefs:** SEO tools that can provide insights into brand visibility on search engines.

CONTENT CREATION & MANAGEMENT:

- **HubSpot and Engagebay:** An all-in-one inbound marketing, sales, and CRM suite. It helps with content creation, distribution, and tracking, ensuring the brand message remains consistent.
- **WordPress:** A widely-used content management system for websites and blogs. With proper themes and plugins, it ensures brand consistency.

FEEDBACK & REVIEW:

- **Uservoice or GetFeedback:** Tools to collect customer feedback, which can be invaluable in refining and adapting brand strategies.

The right combination of these, or similar tools can help in streamlining processes, ensuring brand consistency, and adapting strategies based on data and feedback. It's essential to select tools that align with the studio's specific needs, scale, and budget.

CHAPTER 23

MAXIMIZING YOUR BRAND'S DIGITAL FOOTPRINT

In the digital age, while social media offers invaluable visibility, relying solely on it is insufficient to cement your brand's success. With platforms increasingly throttling external links and prioritizing in-platform content, it becomes paramount to have an accessible digital space of your own: your website. Here's how you can turn your website into a powerhouse for brand success:

Embody Your Brand Identity:

Your website should be more than just a digital platform; it should be an embodiment of your brand's core values and personality. Much like how Neurotic Dog Studios' designs reflect the unique essence of each client, your website should capture the heart and soul of your brand. This includes:

- **Consistent Aesthetics:** Use the same logo, color palette, and design elements across all pages. This reinforces brand recognition, ensuring a unified brand experience.
- **Design Choices:** While eye-catching colors can entice visitors, it's crucial that they serve a purpose. Every design choice, from vibrant hues to the typography used, should resonate with your brand's message. For instance, a serene spa website might opt for soothing blues and simple, elegant fonts, while a fitness brand might lean on bold colors and dynamic design elements.
- **User Experience (UX):** The design should not just be visually appealing but also user-friendly. A clean, minimalistic layout, complemented by strategic pops of brand colors and easily readable fonts, can create a pleasant browsing experience that keeps visitors returning.

Seamless Navigation is Key:

In today's fast-paced digital age, users demand immediacy. A convoluted website structure can deter potential clients or customers.

Here's how to ensure a frictionless browsing experience:

- **Intuitive Structure:** The website's layout should be logical, guiding visitors naturally from one section to another. This ensures they find the information they seek effortlessly, enhancing their association with your brand.
- **Descriptive Navigation Titles:** Labels such as "Services", "Testimonials", or "Contact" immediately inform visitors of the page's content, minimizing guesswork. This clear roadmap encourages deeper site exploration.
- **Search and Sitemaps:** A search function can expedite information retrieval, especially on content-rich sites. Sitemaps, on the other hand, aid both users and search engines. They provide an organized page hierarchy, further simplifying navigation and improving search engine indexing.

Champion Accessibility:

Inclusivity should be at the forefront of modern web design. Everyone, regardless of their abilities, should be able to access and navigate your website with ease. Here's how:

- **Incorporate Alt-Tags and Descriptions:** These assist users with visual impairments by providing context to images. With platforms like WordPress streamlining this process, there's no excuse for overlooking such vital elements.
- **Adaptive Features:** Integrate tools that allow users to modify font size, contrast, or even the site's color scheme. This personalized approach not only improves user experience but also showcases your brand's commitment to inclusivity.
- **Legal and SEO Implications:** Beyond the moral imperative, accessibility now carries legal and SEO ramifications. Search engines prioritize accessible websites, leading to improved organic reach and rankings.

Optimize for Mobile:

The world is increasingly mobile. With smartphones and tablets being primary devices for many, websites must be tailored for smaller screens. Here's how to adapt:

- **Responsive Design:** This ensures your website adjusts its layout based on the device's screen size. Whether a visitor is on a desktop monitor or a smartphone, they'll experience a cohesive brand presentation.
- **Mobile-First Approach:** Some brands opt to design their site for mobile devices first, ensuring optimal performance on these platforms. Given that a significant percentage of users might access your site via mobile, this approach prioritizes their experience.
- **Avoid Over-Complication:** Mobile screens are limited in size. Thus, it's crucial to present information succinctly. Ensure images adjust appropriately, and content remains legible without excessive zooming or scrolling.

Content Freshness Matters:

Just like outdated decor can detract from a physical store's appeal, stale content can diminish your brand's online credibility. Ensuring your site's content remains fresh and relevant is crucial:

- **Regular Audits:** Periodically review site content, removing or updating any outdated information. This ensures visitors always access the most current, accurate information about your brand and its offerings.
- **Automation and Manual Checks:** Leverage tools to automate content updates when possible. However, always complement this with manual reviews to ensure accuracy and alignment with your brand's voice.
- **Customer-Centric Updates:** Ensure that content changes are driven by customer needs. For instance, if a promotion ends, replace it with a new, relevant offer or information, ensuring visitors always find value.

Encourage Interaction:

A static website is a missed opportunity. By fostering two-way communication, you can build deeper relationships with visitors:

- **Interactive Elements:** Embed features like polls, surveys, or comment sections to engage visitors. This transforms passive browsing into an interactive experience, enhancing user engagement and retention.

- **Feedback Loops:** Actively solicit visitor feedback, using it to refine offerings or address concerns. Recognizing and acting on feedback showcases your brand's commitment to continuous improvement.
- **Community Building:** Responding to comments or hosting discussions fosters community. Visitors transform into active brand participants, enhancing loyalty and brand advocacy.

Cultivate Subscribers:

While attracting new visitors is vital, retaining them is equally crucial. Subscriptions turn sporadic visitors into regular audience members:

- **Opt-In Mechanisms:** Encourage site visitors to subscribe to newsletters or updates. This direct line of communication ensures they remain informed about brand happenings, promotions, or new content.
- **Balanced Communication:** While regular updates are valuable, inundating subscribers with daily emails can deter them. Striking a balance ensures they remain engaged without feeling overwhelmed.
- **Legal Compliance:** Ensure your subscription mechanisms adhere to international privacy regulations. This safeguards both your brand and your subscribers, fostering trust and long-term loyalty.

In conclusion, a website isn't just a digital address; it's a dynamic space where your brand story unfolds. It's the space you control, away from the constraints of social media algorithms. Optimize it to resonate with your audience, be accessible to all, and consistently reflect your brand's values. When done right, each of these elements can elevate your website from a mere digital presence to a dynamic brand hub that resonates, engages, and retains its audience.

CHAPTER 24

PLAN AN EFFECTIVE SOCIAL MEDIA MARKETING STRATEGY

Social media serves as a potent tool in the modern branding arsenal. Its universal appeal and accessibility make it an indispensable medium for businesses, irrespective of their domain. Your practice can harness this medium to extend its reach. However, effective social media utilization requires more than sporadic posts or generic content. It necessitates a well-orchestrated strategy.

Define Your Brand Objectives:

Begin by outlining clear objectives. Instead of merely posting images from local events or philanthropic endeavors, each post should reverberate with the brand's ethos. For instance, my branding agency, could share insights on the latest design trends or the significance of branding in healthcare, reflecting its expertise.

Striking the Right Chord: Balancing Education and Entertainment

For health and wellness practitioners, social media is an invaluable platform to reach and educate a vast audience. Yet, the challenge lies in maintaining a delicate equilibrium between providing informative content and engaging users in a way that captivates their attention. Here's how to perfect this balance:

Educate with Authenticity:
- **Articles and Blogs:** Share articles elucidating the benefits of a particular wellness practice, debunking common health myths, or explaining the science behind a specific treatment. For instance, a chiropractor could post an article titled, "Understanding the Science of Spinal Adjustments."
- **Webinars and Live Sessions:** Host live Q&A sessions or webinars on topics like "The Role of Nutrition in Mental Health" or "The Benefits of Meditation for Stress Relief." Real-time interactions can foster trust and deepen patient-practitioner

relationships.
- **Infographics:** Visual summaries of complex topics can be both enlightening and easy to digest. A nutritionist, for example, could share an infographic detailing the "Top 10 Immunity-Boosting Foods."

Engage with Creativity:
- **Patient Testimonials:** Sharing real-life success stories can be incredibly impactful. A physical therapist might showcase a patient's recovery journey after a severe injury through a series of short video clips.
- **Interactive Polls and Quizzes:** Use these to engage your audience and gauge their knowledge. A dietitian could post a quiz titled, "How Well Do You Know Your Superfoods?"
- **Behind-the-Scenes Glimpses:** Offer sneak peeks into a day in the life of a practitioner or a tour of your wellness center. It humanizes the brand and makes it relatable.
- **Memes and Light-hearted Content:** Use humor judiciously to lighten the mood. A meme for a dental clinic might jest, "Eat candy today, visit us tomorrow!" accompanied by a playful image.

Blending Both Worlds:
- **Instructional Videos:** Instead of merely explaining a yoga posture or a meditation technique, create a video tutorial. A "5-minute Morning Yoga Routine" can be both informative and engaging.
- **Interactive Workshops:** Organize online workshops where participants can learn and practice simultaneously. A mental wellness counselor could host a "Mindfulness Meditation Workshop," walking participants through the theory and then guiding a meditation session.
- **Patient Journey Highlights:** Document the transformative journey of a patient. For a weight management clinic, showcasing a patient's weight loss journey, interspersed with their personal challenges, triumphs, workouts, and meal plans, can be deeply inspiring.

In the realm of health and wellness, there's a vast reservoir of content possibilities. The key is to present it in a manner that resonates with your audience's needs and preferences. By blending education with entertainment, health and wellness practitioners can create a compelling narrative that not only informs but also captivates and retains their audience's attention.

Staying Current: Navigating the Fluid Digital Landscape for Health and Wellness Brands

In the digital era, where trends change at lightning speed, it's crucial for brands, especially those in the health and wellness sector, to remain updated and agile. Here's a deeper dive into the significance and strategies to keep your brand contemporary:

The Importance of Staying Current:
- **Relevance:** Brands that align their content with current trends demonstrate their awareness and connectivity to the larger community. For a health and wellness brand, this can translate to sharing the latest research findings, wellness techniques, or fitness challenges.
- **Audience Engagement:** Contemporary content often garners more attention and interaction. For instance, if there's a trending diet or wellness routine, offering professional insights or opinions on it can attract and engage users seeking information.
- **Competitive Edge:** Being one of the first to discuss or adopt a trend can set you apart from competitors. It positions your brand as a frontrunner and thought leader in the industry.

Strategies to Stay Updated:
- **Trend Monitoring Tools:** Use platforms like Google Trends, BuzzSumo, or TrendHunter to keep tabs on trending topics. For health and wellness practitioners, this could be new research on mental health benefits of mindfulness or emerging superfoods.
- **Social Media Listening:** Platforms like Brandwatch or Mention can help monitor online conversations. By listening to what

people are saying about health and wellness, brands can tailor content to address prevalent questions or concerns.

- **Engage with Influencers:** Collaborate with health and wellness influencers who often spearhead or popularize trends. For example, if a renowned fitness influencer introduces a new workout regimen, partnering with them can offer your audience a professional perspective on its benefits and drawbacks.
- **Continual Learning:** Encourage team members to attend webinars, workshops, and conferences. Staying updated with the latest in health and wellness research, innovations, and practices ensures the brand remains a trusted source of information.
- **Feedback Mechanisms:** Engage directly with your audience through surveys, polls, or feedback forms. Understand what topics or trends they're interested in. If a sizable segment expresses curiosity about, say, holistic wellness practices, delve into that area.
- **Adaptability:** While it's crucial to stay current, it's equally vital to ensure the trend aligns with your brand values and objectives. Not every trend will be a fit for every brand. Always assess a trend's relevance to your brand's ethos before jumping on the bandwagon.

Potential Pitfalls:
- **Misinformation:** In the rush to stay updated, ensure that any content shared is accurate and evidence-based, especially in the health and wellness sector where misinformation can have real-world consequences.
- **Overcommitment:** While engaging with multiple trends can seem enticing, it's essential to focus on quality over quantity. Spreading too thin can dilute the brand message and confuse the audience.
- **Authenticity:** Brands should avoid adopting trends that don't align with their core values. Doing so can come off as inauthentic, leading to audience distrust.

The ever-shifting digital terrain offers brands an opportunity to showcase their dynamism and relevance. For health and wellness brands, leveraging this space requires a mix of vigilance, adaptability, and authenticity. By staying current, brands can foster deeper connections, positioning themselves as both contemporaries and leaders in their domain.

Engagement Over Promotion: Cultivating Genuine Conversations on Social Media

The Digital Dialogue:

In an age of digital saturation, mere promotion on social media can often get lost in the noise. Instead, brands need to foster meaningful dialogues. This not only humanizes a brand but also forges deeper, more genuine connections with its audience. For sectors like health and wellness, where trust plays a pivotal role, such engagements become even more critical.

Benefits of Two-Way Communication:
- **Building Trust:** When a brand actively listens and responds, it sends a clear message: "We value your perspective." Over time, this nurtures trust, a cornerstone for any health and wellness entity.
- **Humanizing the Brand:** Engaging conversations help showcase the people behind the brand, making it more relatable and approachable.
- **Gathering Insights:** Direct interactions offer a goldmine of insights about customer preferences, concerns, and feedback, helping in refining services or offerings.
- **Boosting Visibility:** On platforms like Facebook or Instagram, higher engagement rates often translate to better visibility due to algorithmic preferences.

Strategies for Meaningful Engagement:
- **Active Listening:** Monitor mentions, hashtags, or keywords related to your brand. Understand the sentiment and context before responding.

- **Prompt Responses:** Address comments or queries in a timely manner. For health and wellness brands, ensuring that responses are also accurate and evidence-based is crucial.
- **Encourage User-Generated Content (UGC):** Invite your followers to share their experiences or stories. A fitness center might encourage members to post their workout photos or success stories, fostering a sense of community.
- **Host AMAs (Ask Me Anything):** Periodically hosting AMAs with professionals or experts in your domain can drive massive engagement. For example, a nutritionist can host a session on "Demystifying Diet Myths."
- **Polls and Surveys:** Use these tools to solicit opinions on new services, products, or general trends. A wellness retreat center might poll their audience on which workshop they'd prefer next: "Yoga for Stress" or "Meditation Basics."
- **Share Behind-the-Scenes:** Offering glimpses into daily operations, staff introductions, or event preparations can generate organic conversations and make followers feel more connected.
- **Address Negative Feedback Constructively:** Instead of dismissing or avoiding negative comments, address them gracefully, showing commitment to improvement.

Pitfalls to Avoid:
- **Generic Responses:** Avoid canned or repetitive replies. Each response should feel personal and genuine.
- **Over-Promotion:** While it's essential to showcase offerings, every post shouldn't be a sales pitch. Balance is key.
- **Ignoring Feedback:** Not all feedback will be positive. However, ignoring it or, worse, deleting it can harm brand reputation.

Promotion introduces people to a brand, but genuine engagement makes them stay. Especially for health and wellness brands, where personal well-being is at the core, fostering a dialogue that listens, values, and acts upon user interactions is paramount. By prioritizing engagement over mere promotion, brands can cultivate loyalty, trust, and a community of advocatesSelect Platforms Judiciously:

While it's tempting to be omnipresent, it's more effective to dominate a few platforms that resonate with your target audience. Research to discern where your audience primarily interacts and focus your efforts there.

Quality Over Quantity: The Essence of Meaningful Brand Communication

In today's digital age, where the sheer volume of content is staggering, the maxim "less is more" has never been more pertinent. Especially for industries where precision, credibility, and trust are paramount, such as health and wellness, the emphasis on quality content can't be overstated.

The Imperative of Quality:
- **Building Credibility:** Consistently publishing high-quality content establishes a brand as a trustworthy authority in its domain. For health and wellness brands, this trust directly impacts client and patient decisions.
- **Engagement and Retention:** Well-crafted content is more likely to captivate readers, encouraging them to engage with it, share it, and return for more.
- **Optimized Reach:** Search engines prioritize quality content. A well-researched and original article is more likely to rank higher on search engine results, ensuring better visibility and organic reach.
- **Brand Reputation:** In an era where misinformation is rife, especially in health and wellness, consistently delivering quality assures readers of your brand's reliability and commitment to their well-being.

Strategies for Prioritizing Quality:
- **Research Thoroughly:** Before drafting content, invest time in comprehensive research. Rely on credible sources, especially for topics related to health and wellness. For instance, when discussing a new medical treatment, refer to established medical journals or experts in the field.
- **Tailor to Your Audience:** Understand the needs, preferences,

and challenges of your target audience. An article tailored to their concerns will resonate more deeply.

- **Utilize Expert Contributors:** Invite experts or thought leaders in your industry to contribute or review your content. Their insights and endorsements can add immense value.
- **Visual Excellence:** Complement your content with high-quality visuals—images, infographics, or videos. Ensure they are relevant, clear, and professionally crafted.
- **Edit and Review:** Never underestimate the power of revision. Even the best first drafts can benefit from refinement. Ensure clarity, coherence, and accuracy.
- **Gather Feedback:** Encourage your audience to provide feedback. Their insights can help refine content strategy, ensuring it remains relevant and impactful.

Balancing Quality with Frequency:

While quality is paramount, maintaining a consistent posting schedule is also essential. The key is to strike a balance:

- **Content Calendar:** Plan your content in advance. A well-thought-out calendar ensures regular posting while allowing ample time for research and refinement.
- **Repurpose Content:** A comprehensive white paper or study can be broken down into a series of blog posts, infographics, or even short videos. This approach maximizes content reach without compromising quality.
- **Engage with User-Generated Content (UGC):** Encourage your audience to share their stories or experiences. It not only fosters community engagement but also provides authentic content that resonates with peers.

In a world inundated with content, standing out requires more than just volume; it demands value. For brands, especially in health and wellness, prioritizing quality over quantity is not just a choice—it's an imperative. By delivering consistently high-quality content, brands can solidify their reputation, foster trust, and build lasting relationships with their audience.

Crisis Management in the Social Media Era

Navigating the intricacies of social media can be likened to steering a ship through both calm waters and unexpected storms. The instantaneous nature of this digital world, while offering myriad opportunities for brands to engage, also presents the potential for crises to unfold rapidly. Efficient crisis management is crucial, especially for health and wellness brands where trust is paramount.

Understanding Social Media Crises:

A crisis can emerge from various sources:
- **Misinformation or Misinterpretation:** A well-intended post might be misconstrued or taken out of context, leading to backlash.
- **Negative Experiences:** A dissatisfied patient or client might share their grievances, which can quickly gain traction.
- **External Factors:** Events unrelated to your brand, like a general controversy in the health and wellness sector, might inadvertently drag your brand into the discourse.

Steps for Effective Crisis Management:
- **Active Monitoring:** Utilize tools and platforms that notify you of brand mentions, enabling quick responses. For instance, if someone raises concerns about a wellness therapy you promoted, swift acknowledgment is crucial.
- **Prompt Response:** Time is of the essence. Address concerns or criticisms promptly, showcasing your brand's commitment to transparency and accountability.
- **Empathy First:** Respond with understanding and compassion. Avoid defensive or aggressive tones, as they can exacerbate the situation.
- **Fact-based Clarification:** For misunderstandings, provide clear, evidence-backed explanations. If promoting a new wellness practice, citing reputable studies or expert testimonials can dispel misconceptions.
- **Apologize When Necessary:** If a genuine error or oversight occurred, a sincere apology can go a long way in mending

trust.

- **Internal Review:** After addressing the external crisis, conduct an internal review. Understand the root cause to prevent future recurrences.
- **Engage with Advocates:** Mobilize loyal clients or patients who can share positive experiences, helping to balance the narrative.
- **Prepare a Crisis Communication Plan:** Having a pre-established protocol ensures that, in times of crisis, the brand can act swiftly and coherently. This plan should outline communication channels, key spokespersons, and steps for various scenarios.

The Aftermath of a Crisis:

- **Post-Crisis Analysis:** Once the immediate crisis subsides, analyze its origins, the brand's response, and the public's reaction. This analysis provides insights for refining future crisis management strategies.
- **Rebuild and Reconnect:** Invest time in rebuilding any trust that might have been eroded. This might involve outreach campaigns, engaging more closely with the community, or hosting informative sessions to address concerns.
- **Regular Training:** Ensure that all team members, especially those handling social media, undergo regular training on best practices, brand values, and crisis management protocols.

The digital age, with its promise of real-time connectivity, brings both opportunities and challenges for brands. Crisis management, in such a landscape, is less about evading storms and more about adeptly navigating through them. By fostering transparency, empathy, and proactive engagement, health and wellness brands can weather these storms and emerge with even stronger bonds with their community.

Professional Management: The Key to Streamlined Social Media Presence

The dynamic world of social media, with its ever-evolving trends and algorithms, can be daunting for brands, especially those in specialized sectors like health and wellness. While an in-house approach might seem sufficient initially, the value of professional management becomes increasingly evident as brands grow and engagement deepens. Here's why.

The Significance of Professional Management:
- **Expertise & Experience:** Professional social media managers or agencies bring a wealth of knowledge from working with various brands and scenarios. Their experience can be instrumental in charting out successful campaigns, identifying potential pitfalls, and capitalizing on trends.
- **Time Efficiency:** Regularly creating content, monitoring engagements, analyzing metrics, and staying updated with platform changes can be time-consuming. Professionals streamline these tasks, allowing brands to focus on their core services.
- **Consistent Brand Voice:** Professionals ensure that every post, response, and interaction aligns with the brand's voice and ethos. For health and wellness brands maintaining this consistency is crucial in building trust and credibility.
- **Proactive Crisis Management:** Having an expert at the helm means that potential controversies or misunderstandings can be quickly identified and managed before they escalate.
- **Strategic Approach:** A dedicated manager will employ data-driven strategies, regularly analyzing metrics to refine content strategies, optimize post timings, and boost engagement.

Factors to Consider When Opting for Professional Management:
- **Alignment with Brand Vision:** Whether hiring an individual or partnering with an agency, ensure they resonate with the brand's mission and values. A deep understanding of the brand's objectives and target audience is paramount.
- **Portfolio Review:** Before onboarding, review their past work, particularly for brands in the health and wellness sector. This provides insights into their style, expertise, and adaptability.
- **Regular Communication:** Establish clear channels of

communication. Regular updates, feedback sessions, and strategy discussions ensure that both the brand and the manager are on the same page.

- **Budget Considerations:** While professional management is an investment, it's essential to find a balance between cost and quality. Determine a clear budget, but also recognize the value that expert management brings.
- **Flexibility & Adaptability:** Social media is fluid, and what works today might not tomorrow. Ensure that the chosen professional is adaptable, willing to innovate, and not rigidly tied to a single approach.

Social media, as a potent tool for brand visibility and engagement, demands a nuanced approach. While brands might initially manage their presence independently, as the complexity and stakes grow, the advantages of professional management become clear. By partnering with experts, brands can navigate the digital landscape more effectively, ensuring their message resonates clearly, consistently, and impactfully.

Diverse Content: Crafting a Rich and Varied Digital Tapestry

In the vast digital arena, capturing and retaining attention is both an art and a science. A monotonous content stream can deter even the most loyal followers, while a varied and vibrant showcase can draw in and engage diverse audience segments. Here's a deeper dive into the importance of content diversity and how to implement it effectively, especially for sectors like health and wellness.

Why Diverse Content Matters:
- **Catering to Varied Preferences:** Different audience segments consume content differently. While some prefer in-depth articles, others might be drawn to visuals or quick video snippets. Offering a variety ensures you cater to a broad spectrum.
- **Enhanced Engagement:** Mixing content types can break monotony, ensuring your audience remains engaged and curious about what's coming next.

- **Optimized Platform Use:** Different social platforms favor different content types. Instagram, for example, is visually-driven, while LinkedIn might favor more in-depth articles or posts.

Diversifying Content - A Closer Look:

ARTICLES & BLOG POSTS:
- **Purpose:** Ideal for in-depth exploration of topics, sharing insights, or providing valuable information.
- **Tips:** Keep the language simple and relatable. Utilize headings, bullet points, and infographics for better readability. For health and wellness, topics might include "The Benefits of Meditation" or "Understanding Dietary Supplements."

IMAGES & GRAPHICS:
- **Purpose:** Visuals can convey messages quickly, evoke emotions, or highlight specific brand aspects.
- **Tips:** Use high-resolution images. Ensure any text overlays are legible. Infographics can be especially useful in the health sector to break down complex topics like "The Anatomy of a Balanced Diet."

VIDEOS:
- **Purpose:** Ideal for tutorials, behind-the-scenes glimpses, or storytelling.
- **Tips:** Keep videos concise but informative. Ensure good audio quality. For health and wellness practitioners, videos could cover topics like exercise demonstrations or patient testimonials.

INTERACTIVE CONTENT (QUIZZES, POLLS, ETC.):
- **Purpose:** Engage the audience actively, gather insights, or simply entertain.
- **Tips:** Ensure the content aligns with brand objectives. For instance, a wellness center might post a quiz titled "Which Yoga Routine is Right for You?"

Maintaining Quality Across Content Types:
- **Copyright Compliance:** Always ensure that visuals or other content used are either original, purchased, or free from copyright restrictions. Inadvertent violations can lead to legal complications and harm brand reputation.
- **Consistency in Branding:** Whether it's an article, image, or video, ensure that elements like color schemes, logos, or tone remain consistent, reinforcing brand identity.
- **Feedback Loop:** Encourage audience feedback on content types and topics. Their insights can guide future content strategies.

Diverse content is not just about variety for its own sake. It's a strategic approach to engage, educate, and resonate with a multifaceted audience. By weaving a rich tapestry of articles, visuals, videos, and interactive content, brands can ensure a dynamic and vibrant digital presence, making every touchpoint an opportunity for meaningful connection.

Select Platforms Judiciously: Navigating the Social Media Landscape with Precision

The allure of the vast social media universe can be overwhelming. With a plethora of platforms, each offering unique features and audience demographics, the decision of where to mark a brand's presence becomes critical. Especially for sectors like health and wellness, it's not just about where you speak, but who listens and engages.

Why Platform Selection Matters:
- **Audience Alignment:** Every platform caters to distinct audience demographics. For instance, while Instagram might be popular among millennials seeking fitness inspiration, LinkedIn could be apt for B2B engagement in the healthcare domain.
- **Resource Optimization:** Effective social media management demands time, effort, and often, financial resources. Focusing on select platforms ensures better resource allocation and

impact.

- **Message Delivery:** The format and tone that resonate on TikTok might differ vastly from what's appropriate for Facebook. Choosing platforms aligned with your content style ensures the message is both heard and appreciated.

Steps to Prudent Platform Selection:
- **Audience Research:** Understand where your potential patients or clients spend their time. For a pediatric wellness clinic, platforms popular among parents, like Facebook or parenting forums, might be apt.
- **Analyze Current Trends:** Stay updated with the latest social media trends. If there's a surge in health-related podcasts, platforms supporting audio content might be worth exploring.
- **Assess Content Suitability:** If your strategy leans heavily towards video content, platforms like YouTube or Instagram become natural choices. On the other hand, for article-heavy content, LinkedIn or a personal blog might be more appropriate.
- **Evaluate Engagement Potential:** Some platforms foster deeper interactions through comments, shares, or direct messages. For health and wellness brands that prioritize community-building, such platforms can be invaluable.
- **Pilot and Pivot:** Before a full-fledged dive, consider piloting your presence on a new platform. Monitor engagement, gather feedback, and assess alignment with brand objectives.

Balancing Breadth and Depth:

While it's essential to diversify, diving deep into a few platforms can sometimes yield better results than a shallow presence across many. For instance, a holistic wellness brand might prioritize depth on Instagram, offering a mix of posts, IGTV videos, stories, and live sessions, while maintaining a more minimalistic presence on X (formerly Twitter).

Social media strategy is as much about where you communicate as it is about what you communicate. In the health and wellness domain, where trust, credibility, and personal touch are paramount, selecting the right platforms becomes the foundation of a robust digital strategy. As we wind up this chapter, remember: it's not about echoing in the vastness but resonating in the right chambers.

PART 6

References & Resources

""Your brand is a story unfolding across all customer touchpoints."

– Jonah Sachs,
author and branding expert

Jonah Sachs is an acclaimed author, speaker, and branding expert known for his insightful perspectives on storytelling and brand strategy. With a profound understanding of the power of storytelling in shaping perceptions and driving meaningful connections, Sachs has become a sought-after voice in the world of branding. He is the author of "Winning the Story Wars" and has contributed to numerous publications, including The New York Times and Fast Company. Through his work, Sachs emphasizes the importance of creating authentic and purpose-driven narratives that resonate with audiences on a deeper level. He believes that successful brands are those that inspire, engage, and align with the values and aspirations of their customers. Sachs's expertise has helped businesses leverage the power of storytelling and purpose to build stronger, more meaningful connections with their audiences, ultimately driving brand loyalty and success.

Alice Pettey

ABOUT THE AUTHOR

I don't know about you, but the "about" section is one that I have always hated to write.

I mean, really, what do you what to know or even care about? Should I list my credentials and accolades? They can sound great, right? But, then again, that could just sound pompous and egotistical & hey, do you really care that I graduated Valedictorian of my Master's program or that I'm a certified brand strategist? Maybe, what you really want is how I got here and the why behind it all. It's not an exciting story. It definitely, has a bit of tragedy and frustration woven through, but if you're up for it & want to know, here goes.

WHERE DOES THE STORY START?

I guess after college makes sense. Of course, by then, I'd already set aside my dreams for the realities of having two children to support. Nothing revolutionary here, just youthful spur-of-the-moment decisions that result in lifelong consequences – you know, life. But, it did lead me into my first full-time position with an interior design agency.

I worked as the receptionist/office manager for the firm but was exposed to a new world of experience. Not in designing office layouts but in the technology used. This I found fascinating. So just two years out from getting my Bachelor of Arts (in History, no less), I enrolled in courses for Graphic Design & Multimedia Design. This was way back in 1999, but I found programs I could take fully online.

Once I got a foundation for the software and the basics of design concepts, I dug in deep through books, training programs, videos, seminars, and anything else that I could think of that would help expand my understanding of design and creativity. I learned that there was design, and then there was DESIGN. Anyone can do design.

Today, that's what Canva is for – making design accessible & it's great. It provides templates and frameworks to non-designers to create pieces that look good & fulfill their needs without having to devote the hours and expense of hiring or learning design. But then there is DESIGN. This is not about making things look nice – this is about approaching things from a strategic and business focus. It's about communication and fulfilling business goals.

Here I am all excited about this new thing, "strategic design," and how it needs to be brought into the process SO much earlier and not seen as the afterthought to make things pretty. But 9-11 happens, and businesses downsize, and as I'm expecting my third child, I'm an easy layoff. It was a fun Christmas that year. But, come April, we welcomed our youngest son into the family, and life was never the same.

A SHIFT IN FOCUS AND CHANGE IN PRIORITIES

Our youngest son came with some surprises. We discovered over the course of his first three years that our baby had Smith-Magenis Syndrome. Our simple explanation is "Autism on steroids," but there is so much more to it; if you're interested, check out PRISMS.org.

With this diagnosis, the direction of our entire family's life changed. The husband and I spent a week in mourning. No one really tells you that. You actually mourn when you get that kind of life-altering diagnosis. You mourn the life you thought you and/or your child were going to have. The plans you made, the dream you didn't eave realize you had. Our son wasn't quite three when he was diagnosed, but it's amazing how much of his future I had already dreamed.

Our daughter, four at our youngest birth, responded by becoming a little mommy. And she was, right up until the day he died while she & her father tried to save him.

Our oldest son withdrew into himself and suffered severe depression – that we missed because of the constant focus on our youngest. Thankfully, he's still with us.

During the 18 years we had with our youngest; we were blessed with his love, isolated by his condition, ostracized by lack of understanding of his behaviors; restricted by obligation & devotion; resentful of limitations; guilt-ridden for our frustration and resentments; overwhelmed by it all, and trying to present a normal exterior to the world.

I explored so many healing modalities. In another life, I would have gone into that field, but the time and energy required to truly master any of them takes a lifetime, and I recognize my limitations. That is why I respect those who devote themselves to helping others so much. Western medicine definitely has its place, but I do so wonder, if we could have invested more into it, would eastern medicine have been able to make our son's life better? Would it have provided a way to have lessened the locked door that he was trapped behind?

I have so much anger at one of our local hospitals. We were there a week before our son's passing for pre-op (he'd had a dental abscess for 4+ months that they were finally going to address, and given his condition, required an OR); during this check-up, his extremity pulse-ox was 52. I'd never seen them take one on the forehead before – but they managed to get a peak at 93, though typically even that stayed in the 80s & they cleared him for surgery.

Of course, it didn't matter. A week later, we showed up for surgery, and he didn't want to go in. The hospital REFUSED to assist us in getting him into the facility. My husband fought with him for 45 minutes, and I begged for help inside. Finally, we left, and he was dead by mid-afternoon the next day. – I am A-N-G-E-R-Y.

But, angry or not, it will not bring my son back. So here I am; two years have passed since his death, and I'm trying to make sense of it. What to do with my life, and how I can use my skills to make the world a better place in his memory.

FOCUS AND STRATEGY FOR THE FUTURE

I know branding – Think about your best friend, your spouse, and your significant other. Think about what makes them – them. What they wear. What they listen to. What they sound like. What they smell like. What makes them laugh? What makes them cry? When you walk through a store, there are things that are going to make you instantly think of them. You have that recognition – that's branding.

It's the conversation, the chance to find clarity, to understand whom you are actually trying to reach, the concepts – the strategy – behind who you are and why you do what you do. It's not about making it pretty. It's about reaching the right people. It's about understanding why you get up in the morning and go to your practice. It's about understanding whom you're trying to help and why you're trying to help them. It's about communicating that message to them on a daily basis. Solving their problems and letting them know what those problems are before they even realize they have them.

It is innate for every person – on an unconscious, visceral level to understand and connect with another person. What brand strategists do is help translate that from individual to individual to your company. To help you develop a visceral experience for the right people. You're not going to be the right practitioner for everyone, and you're not going to be the practitioner for most, but there are the right people, and for those right people, there will never be another practitioner who could replace you. Those are the people we need to make connections with, and yeah, some of it is the down-and-dirty bit, known as marketing and sales, that gets their attention, but it's the branding that keeps them.

I see your frustration, and I have experienced that same frustration myself. I know that together we can connect you with the people who will not only benefit from the services that you can bring to them but will appreciate what you can do.

So now, my purpose, is to connect you with the right people and the right clients so that your frustration levels decline and your practices succeed. That your practice becomes more profitable and more fulfilling, and that you are servicing the group of individuals you are meant for to serve. And maybe, just maybe, people like my son won't get lost in the shuffle because there will be more people like you, with the time, resources, energy and skills who care.

Special Offers

FREE BRANDING CONSULTATION

Thank you for taking the time to read, and hopefully work through, *Branding Your Practice*. If you've found that you'd like to have a bit more assistance than this book provides I'd love to talk with you!

With our mission to support health and wellness practitioners in standing out and making meaningful connections with their communities, we are always looking for ways to contribute and make a difference.

I am thrilled to extend an exclusive offer to you: A **Complimentary Branding Consultation** with me, Alice Pettey, the founder of Neurotic Dog Studios. This session will provide insights into how a robust branding strategy can elevate your practice, help distinguish you from competitors, and create a visceral experience for your target audience.

What to Expect from the Consultation:
- A deep dive into your current brand identity, its strengths, and areas of improvement.
- Discussions on your vision, mission, and the experience you wish to convey to your clients or patients.
- Initial insights and recommendations on branding strategies tailored to your specific needs.

We, at Neurotic Dog Studios, firmly believe that the right branding can work wonders, forging bonds that feel nothing short of magical. I am confident that this session will shed light on potential avenues to amplify your brand's resonance and reach.

To redeem this offer, please visit **zcal.co/meetNDS** to schedule your consultation. We are excited about the prospect of collaborating with you and embarking on a journey to refine and rejuvenate your brand identity.

Warm Regards,

Alice Pettey
Founder

NEUROTIC DOG
STUDIOS

P.S.   Looking for more information??   Check out Differentiate Magazine. It's a quarterly magazine that is focused on helping health and wellness practitioners brand and grow their practice. Inside Differentiate you'll find branding, marketing, social media, practice culture, technology tips and more. All geared towards you—the health and wellness practice owner.

www.differentiatemag.com

Appendix A: Target Audience Persona Worksheet

Target Audience Persona Worksheet

Persona Information

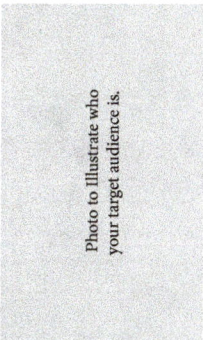

Persona's (made up) Name: _____

Geographic Location: _____

Age: _____

Gender: _____

Educational Level: _____

Income: _____

Occupation: _____

Faith/Religious Beliefs: _____

_____

_____

_____

Target Demographics (*Target Attributes*)

Family (Single? Married? Children? Pets?): _____

Social Life (Hobbies? Dining Out? Outdoor Activities? etc.): _____

Social Media (Facebook user? X (formerly Twitter)? Other?): _____

Cultural (Book reader? Music lover? Art lover? etc.): _____

Political: _____

Ethnicity: _____

Personal Values (core beliefs worth fighting for): _____

Clubs/Tribes (Starbucks loyalist? Fitness enthusiast? Smartphone user? etc): _____

Photo to Illustrate who your target audience is.

Target Persona's Story

(use the Information above to write a 200–250 word narrative of your persona)

_____

_____

_____

_____

_____

_____

_____

_____

_____

_____

_____

Appendix B: Elements of Branding

Simplified Structure of Brand Elements

BRANDING						
BRAND STRATEGY	**Purpose - The Why**			**POSITIONING**		
	Vision	Mission	Values	Target Audience	Competitors	Difference
BRAND EXPRESSION	**CHARACTER**		**VERBAL EXPRESSION**		**VISUAL EXPRESSION**	
	Personality	Brand Voice	Core Message	Story Telling	Name | Tagline | Promise	Visual Identity	Presence
	REPUTATION					

INTERNAL CULTURE	
COMMITMENTS	
CONSISTANCY	TRUST

Comprehensive View of Elements that Make up Branding

BRANDING

HUMAN CENTE

VALUES		NEEDS	
Values	Purpose	Voice	Persona

BELIEFS	VISION	MISSION	VALUES

BRAND STRATEGY

INTERNAL BRAND

SECONDARY CORE MESSAGE

Vision	Mission	Values
Someday	Everyday	
NAVIGATION	RULEBOOK	

Causes — Emotional Connection

Purpose - The Why		
Meaningful	Difference	Destiny	Liberating
INNER BELIEF		ALIGNED BELIEFS	
Positive Culture	Camaraderie	Fosters Connection	Builds Trust

POSITIONING

Audience		Offering	

POSITIONING STATEMENT (PRIMARY CORE MESSAG

WHO?	WHAT?	HOW?	WHEN?	WHERE?
Target Audience		Competitors	Differe
Pain Points	Key Benefits	Compet. Altern.	Diff. Sta
Emotional Connection	Causes	Analysis	Gaps	Wo
Purpose Behind the Cause	Who/what is being helped	Strenths Weaknesses	Due Dille
Understanding	Resonates	Research	
		Unique Offering	
Audience Persona			
Demographics	Psychographics		
Statistical Data	Behaviors/Interests	BRAND	ON

INTERNAL CULTURE

PURPOSE	VALUES	BEHAVIORS	RECOGNITION	RITUALS
A grand vision of why an organization exists beyond making money.	Words, phrases, and symbols that represent shared beliefs about what is most important when conducting business. They guide the choices that individuals make within an organization as they strive to achieve a set of shared goals.	Choices made by employees that are guided by purpose Behaviors begin with strategy. Leadership: Do=Say; Say=Do Culture is not shaped by one choice, but 10,000 decisions.	Programs that applaud and encourage behaviors that support the culture. Types: Formal Leadership | Informal Leadership | Formal Peer | Informal Peer || All must be identified and recognized to encourage culture growth	Activities that build an strengthen relationshi Types: 1. Explicit Big Rituals 2. Explicit Sn Rituals 3. Emergent Group Rituals 4. Em Big Group Rituals

C

CONSISTANCY	
Specific Group	

NEUROTIC DOG STUDIOS

RAND		
CARES	WANTS	
Message	Story	Look & Feel

ITY				
Y	CHARACTERISTICS	TONE OF VOICE	CONVERSATION STYLE	POLITICAL POSITION

BRAND EXPRESSION

ARACTER	VERBAL EXPRESSION			VISUAL EXPRESSION		REPUTATION			
ty | Brand Voice	Core Message	Story Telling	Name | Tagline | Promise	Visual Identity	Presence	Online Media	Print Media	Public Relations	
increase the value	What You Want Your Audience to Understand	Trust Empathy Cooperation	From Positioning	Standards		Social Media	Website	Press Releases	Crisis Management
great intangibles				-Logo -Color		Posts	Videos	Articles	Announcements

Brand Voice column:
- Belonging
- Centrality
- Symbolism
- Simplicity
- Delight
- Protection
- Safety
- Flexibility

Positioning

What You Say	How You Say It
- Marketing	
- Website Copy	
- Social Posts	
- Advertisements	
- Press Resleases	
- Collateral	
- Packaging	
- Emails	
- Visual Identity	
- Brand Expression	

Primary	Secondary
1 - Simplicity	
2 - Emotion	
3 - Personality	

Visual Identity Standards:
-Logo   -Color
-Images   -Type
-Patterns -Style
-Lighting -Place

BRAND STORY
Copywriting

1–Write Ugly First	2–Write As Your Brand Persona	3–Write to Your Audience Persona	4–Drop The Jargon	5–Inject Action
Brand Purpose Statement	Vocabulary		Use Familiar Terminology	VERBS Think, Play, Act, Do, Give, Take, Achieve, Learn
Core Message	Language		Undertandable	
	Attitudes			
Sales Page	Characteristics		Clear	ADJECTIVES Intensely, Extremely, Fluffy
	Opinions			

CUES column:
al and behavioral
hat help employees
and leaders stay
to the future. Types
mediate Cues
pirational Cues
mmediate Cues
Aspirational Cues

ENTS	
TRUST	
	Feeling

Appendix C: Typography Websites

www.myfonts.com

www.creativemarket.com

www.hypefortype.com

www.linotype.com

www.fonts.com

www.fontshop.com

www.fontfont.com

www.typography.com

www.fontspring.com

www.veer.com/products/fonts/

www.houseind.com/fonts/

www.fontsquirrel.com

www.1001fonts.com/free-fonts-
for-commercial-use.html

For a fairly comprehensive list of foundries world wide visit:
http://type-foundries-archive.com/

Appendix D: Types of Internal Communication

Leadership communication
- [ ] Town hall announcements
- [ ] Employee newsletters sent on behalf of leadership
- [ ] Progress reports
- [ ] KPI overviews
- [ ] Company-wide message over intranet

Peer-to-peer communication
- [ ] Staff social media spaces and slack
- [ ] Virtual town halls
- [ ] Interactive employee newsletters
- [ ] Virtual weekly stand-up meetings

Change management communication
- [ ] Employee newsletters with feedback features
- [ ] Face-to-face virtual meetings with Q&A sessions
- [ ] Your virtual town hall
- [ ] Intranet communications

Culture communication
- [ ] First and foremost—your internal company newsletter
- [ ] On-boarding communications
- [ ] All and any virtual events

Bottom-up conversations
- [ ] Discussion forums such as slack channels and Microsoft Teams groups
- [ ] Staff blogs and social media tools
- [ ] Suggestion boxes and pulse surveys
- [ ] Virtual focus groups

New hire communication
- [ ] Personalized employee on-boarding newsletters
- [ ] One-on-one biweekly meetings
- [ ] Employee pulse surveys

Health and safety communication
- [ ] Your on-boarding communications
- [ ] Health and safety policy employee handbook promoted and attached via employee newsletters
- [ ] Safety training videos on your company's YouTube or embedded in internal emails

Company updates

- [ ] Employee newsletters with scheduling features so you can prepare content in advance
- [ ] Set up weekly one-on-one virtual meetings where each employee can ask questions individually
- [ ] Use anonymous feedback and question tools so employees can voice concerns or ask questions they may feel embarrassed discussing publicly

Campaign communication

- [ ] Internal emails
- [ ] Slack and other team messaging groups
- [ ] Your intranet
- [ ] Virtual meetings and events

Employee recognition communication

- [ ] Digital thank you notes— personalized emails to employees expressing gratitude for specific accomplishments
- [ ] A virtual town hall segment dedicated to leaders recognizing standout employees
- [ ] An employee appreciation video embedded into your internal newsletter

Crisis communication

- [ ] Pre-planned and easily accessible crisis handbook or guide for health and safety-related emergencies
- [ ] External and internal social media channels such as X (formerly Twitter) and any staff blogs or forums
- [ ] Company newsletter designated for crisis discussion and feedback
- [ ] Pulse surveys and anonymous comments in employee emails so they can express individual concerns
- [ ] Company intranet

Employee Wellness communication

- [ ] Employee newsletters
- [ ] Pulse surveys on employee wellness
- [ ] Virtual focus groups on employee health and wellness

Holiday communication

- [ ] Holiday-themed employee newsletters
- [ ] A holiday video featuring a thoughtful message from your leadership team
- [ ] Holiday segment in your virtual town hall

Diversity and inclusion communication

- [ ] Newsletters promoting D&I initiatives and mentor-ship groups
- [ ] Internal email dedicated to outlining your diversity and inclusion policies
- [ ] Diversity and inclusion pulse surveys
- [ ] Meetings designated for D&I training

Event management communication

- [ ] Interactive newsletters by adding GIFs in your Outlook emails, insert emojis, and feature feedback options.
- [ ] An email tool with embedded event registration and tracking like ContactMonkey's event management tool.
- [ ] Save the date alerts on your staff social media.

Appendix E: Employee Communication Survey Questions

Information Flow

- Do you get the information you need when you need it?
- How would you rate your awareness of the company's goals?
- Do you know how your work helps the company meet its goals and objectives?
- How do you typically get information about the company?
- How would you prefer to get information about the company?
- How would you rate your direct manager's efforts to keep you informed?
- Does the organization provide adequate information about your progress in your job?
- Does the organization provide adequate information about its policies and goals?
- Does the organization provide adequate information about critical changes?
- How can our company improve communications?
- What company communication pathway do you find to be the most ineffective?
- How well are you informed about how our company is performing?

Organizational Transparency

- How transparent do you feel management is with you?
- Do senior members of the organization regularly share views on issues of importance?
- What is your level of understanding of the long-term competitive strategy of the organization?
- Do departments in the organization communicate frequently with each other?
- Do you feel that the company always tells the truth?
- Does the company provide accurate information to you?
- How would you rate the level of communication you get from the company?

Social Media

- Does the organization's internal use of social media improve communication between you and your colleagues?
- Does the company's internal use of social media give you a sense of belonging and community?
- Does the organization's internal use of social media give you a way to influence the company?

Recognition

- Do you feel valued in the workplace?
- How well does our company culture drive your engagement in your work?
- Have you received recognition from a manager in the past two weeks?
- Does our organization do a good job of promoting recognition in the workplace?
- How well are you recognized for your great work?

Feedback

- Do you feel that the company takes your concerns and feedback seriously?
- How would you rate our organization's actions on your previous feedback?
- Do you see any positive change since we started collecting employee feedback?

Appendix F: Monthly Content Calendar

Month: _____

Year: _____

1. Content Idea: _____

_____

Publication Platform:

☐ *Events:* ☐ Speaking Engagement ☐ Live Streams ☐ Webinar
            ☐ Podcast

☐ *Social Media:* ☐ YouTube   ☐ LinkedIn   ☐ Instagram
            ☐ X (formerly Twitter)   ☐ Facebook

☐ *Print:* ☐ Newsletter   ☐ White Papers   ☐ Magazine

☐ *Public Relation:* ☐ Press Release ☐ Announcement ☐ Outreach
            ☐ Speech

☐ *Other:* _____

Type: ☐ Video ☐ Carousel ☐ Feed Post ☐ Story/Short ☐ Article
            ☐ Podcast

Publication (Live) Date: _____

Internal Due Date: _____

Assignee: _____

2. Content Idea: _____

_____

Publication Platform:

☐ *Events:* ☐ Speaking Engagement ☐ Live Streams ☐ Webinar
            ☐ Podcast

☐ *Social Media:* ☐ YouTube   ☐ LinkedIn   ☐ Instagram
            ☐ X (formerly Twitter)   ☐ Facebook

☐ *Print:* ☐ Newsletter   ☐ White Papers   ☐ Magazine

☐ *Public Relation:* ☐ Press Release ☐ Announcement ☐ Outreach
☐ Speech

☐ *Other:* _____

Type: ☐ Video ☐ Carousel ☐ Feed Post ☐ Story/Short ☐ Article
☐ Podcast

Publication (Live) Date: _____

Internal Due Date: _____

Assignee: _____

3. Content Idea: _____

_____

Publication Platform:

☐ *Events:* ☐ Speaking Engagement ☐ Live Streams ☐ Webinar
☐ Podcast

☐ *Social Media:* ☐ YouTube ☐ LinkedIn ☐ Instagram
☐ X (formerly Twitter) ☐ Facebook

☐ *Print:* ☐ Newsletter ☐ White Papers ☐ Magazine

☐ *Public Relation:* ☐ Press Release ☐ Announcement ☐ Outreach
☐ Speech

☐ *Other:* _____

Type: ☐ Video ☐ Carousel ☐ Feed Post ☐ Story/Short ☐ Article
☐ Podcast

Publication (Live) Date: _____

Internal Due Date: _____

Assignee: _____

Appendix G: Content/Marketing Calendar

Month: _____ Year: _____

Saturday					
Friday					
Thursday					
Wednesday					
Tuesday					
Monday					
Sunday					

Appendix H: Competitor Bulls Eye Diagram

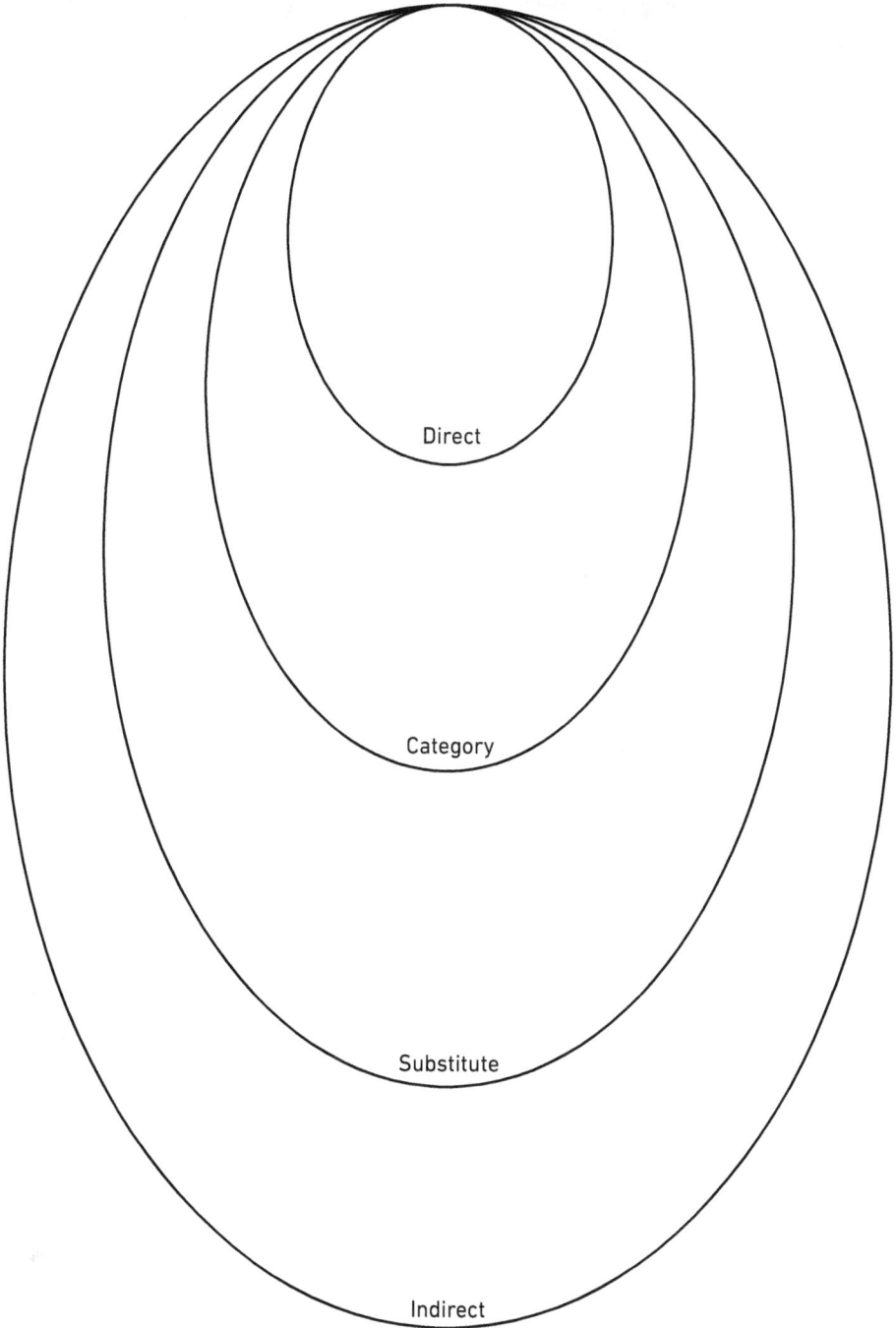

Direct

Category

Substitute

Indirect

Appendix I: Top Competitors

Competitor Name	What do they do well?	What do you do better?

Appendix J: How Is Your Brand Unique?

Differentiate

The most valuable companies know why they exist. Over time, the what and how you do things changes, but the Why does not.

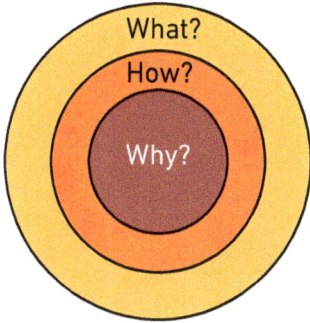

*"People don't buy **what** you do, they buy **why** you do it."*

— Simon Sinek

Explain your:

Why? _____

_____

_____

_____

How? _____

_____

_____

_____

What? _____

_____

_____

_____

Appendix K: Brand Style Attribute Scale

Place a mark on each scale to indicate where the brand fall for each pair of attributes.

CLASSIC ———————————————————————————— MODERN

ECONOMICAL ———————————————————————————— LUXURIOUS

FEMININE ———————————————————————————— MASCULINE

PLAYFUL ———————————————————————————— SERIOUS

ROUND ———————————————————————————— SHARP

Appendix L: SWOT Matrix

SWOT MATRIX Strengths & Weaknesses are "Internal" Opportunities and Threats are "External" Create strategies for the intersection of the S & W with the O & T	STRENGTHS	WEAKNESSES
OPPORTUNITIES	S/O STRATEGIES	W/O STRATEGIES
THREATS	S/T STRATEGIES	W/T STRATEGIES

Appendix M: 210 Brand Attribute Terms

Innovative	Nurturing	Dexterous
Trustworthy	Curious	Multifaceted
Authentic	Revolutionary	Diligent
Professional	Seamless	Celebrated
Friendly	Adaptive	Noble
Dynamic	Elegant	Majestic
Accessible	Cohesive	Exquisite
Empowering	Charismatic	Lavish
Premium	Spirited	Jubilant
Passionate	Tenacious	Vibrant
Transparent	Proactive	Gracious
Sustainable	Harmonious	Benevolent
Versatile	Discerning	Renowned
Resilient	Cultured	Iconic
Pioneering	Balanced	Reputable
Holistic	Diverse	Stalwart
Ethical	Progressive	Pragmatic
Collaborative	Grounded	Rational
Empathetic	Traditional	Thoughtful
User-centric	Ambitious	Mindful
Global	Noble	Consistent
Inclusive	Robust	Enduring
Modern	Zesty	Flourishing
Energetic	Wholesome	Vital
Intuitive	Crafted	Joyful
Refined	Radiant	Encouraging
Loyal	Warm	Valiant
Adventurous	Serene	Synergetic
Efficient	Assertive	Placid
Inspiring	Gratifying	Uplifting
Reliable	Enlightening	Resonant
Transformative	Aesthetic	Memorable
Timeless	Genuine	Pristine
Visionary	Committed	Urbane

Pleasurable
Bountiful
Agile
Charming
Delightful
Esteemed
Polished
Flourishing
Tranquil
Resolute
Invigorating
Tactile
Luminous
Tangible
Fulfilling
Revered
Elite
Fastidious
Disciplined
Opulent
Thriving
Captivating
Enriching
Rewarding
Festive
Panoramic
Enigmatic
Sumptuous
Legendary
Epicurean
Masterful
Eloquent
Sterling
Superior
Auspicious
Honorable

Lucid
Stimulating
Valuable
Resplendent
Affluent
Grandeur
Fascinating
Sublime
Lustrous
Radiant
Finesse
Plush
Luxurious
Paramount
Regal
Dominant
Salient
Majestic
Quintessential
Swanky
Conclusive
Laudable
Peerless
Slick
Idyllic
Prestigious
Striking
Compelling
Acclaimed
Distinguished
Consummate
Exemplary
Unsurpassed
Optimal
Elite
Ultimate

Matchless
Sensational
Stupendous
Prolific
Unbeatable
Prime
Top-tier
Monumental
Classy
Transcendent
Chief
Superb
Peerless
Leading
Predominant
Incomparable
Unrivaled
Supreme
Exceptional
Premier
Virtuoso
Stellar
Top-notch
Superior
Outstanding
Foremost
Multifaceted
Trailblazing
Tenacious
Whimsical
Meticulous
Magnetic
Visionary
Groundbreaking
Pragmatic
Timeless

Appendix N: Brand Attribute Worksheet

Fill in each column utilizing term from Appendix M: Brand Attributes, or come up with your own.

CULTURE	COMMUNITY	VOICE	FEELING	IMPACT	X-FACTOR
How would your community describe you?	How would you describe your patients/ community?	How do you sound to others?	How others feel after interacting with you?	What tangible impact do you have on others?	How are you different from others? What makes you special?

Once done – select the three best terms from each column > then move to 1 for each. These are your brand attributes, and should be reflected in all of your branding and marketing materials.

Bibliography

Aaker, David A. *Building Strong Brands.* 1996. The Free Press. New York.

Adair. John. *The Art of Creative Thinking: How to be Innovative and Develop Great Ideas.* 2007. Kogan Page Limited. Philadelphia, London.

Airey, David. *Logo Design Love: a guide to creating iconic brand identities.* 2010. New Riders. Berkley.

Albert, Kevin. *Branding Secrets: The Underground Playbook for Building A Great Brand with Very Little Money.* 2021.

Altman, Eli. *Don't Call It That.* 2013. ExtraCurricular Press. San Franscisco.

Budelmann, Kevin & Kim, Yang. *Brand Identity Essentials: 100 Principles for Building Brands.* 2019. Quarto Publishing Group. Beverly.

Cherry, Paul. *Questions that Sell: The Powerful Process for Discovering What Your Customer Really Wants, Second Edition.* 2006. AMACOM. New York

Dayal, Sandeep. *Branding between the Ears: Using Cognitive science to build Lasting Customer Connections.* 2022. McGraw-Hill Education.

Dollins, Mark & Stemmle, Jon. *Engaging Employees Through Strategic Communication: Skills, Strategies, and Tactics.* 2022. Routledge.

Felton, G. *Advertising Concept and Copy, second ed.* 2006. W.W. Norton & Company. New York, London

Geyrhalter, Fabian. *How to Launch a Brand, Second Edition.* 2016. Brandtro Publishing. Long Beach.

Godin, Seth. *Permission Marketing: turning strangers into friends, and friends into customers.* 1999. Simon & Schuster. New York.

Goodson, Scott. *Uprising: How to build a brand—and change the world—by sparking cultural movements.* 2012. McGraw-Hill.

Gray, Haley. *Fearless Marketing: Your 8-Figure Business Blueprint: Marketing doesn't have to be a mystery.* 2018. ICK Publishing.

Gray, Kyle. *The Story Engine: An Entrepreneur's Guide to Content Strategy and Brand Storytelling Without Spending All Day Writing.* 2016.

Hartwell, Margaret. *Archetypes in Branding: A toolkit for creatives and strategists*

Johnson, Michael. *Branding In Five And A Half Steps.* 2016. Thames & Hudson. New York.

Keller, Kevin Lane & Swaminathan, Vanitha. *Strategic Brand Management: Building, Measuring and Managing Brand Equity. Fifth Edition.* 2008. Pearson. Hoboken.

Levine, Josh. *Great Mondays: How to design a company culture employees love.* 2019. McGraw-Hill Education. New York.

Middleton, Simon. *Build A Brand in 30 Days.* 2010. Capstone Publishing Ltd. Chichester, West Sussex.

Miller, Donald. *Marketing Made Simple: A Step-By-Step Storybrand Guide for any Business.* 2020. HarperCollins Leadership.

Miller, Donald. *Building A Story Brand:*

Clarify Your Message so Customers Will Listen. 2017. HarperCollins Leadership.

Mitchel, Colin, *Selling the Brand Inside.* January 2002. Harvard Business Review.

Motherbaugh, David L., Hawkins, Del I., & Kleiser, Susan Bardi. *Consumer Behavior: Building Marketing Strategy, Fourteenth Edition.* 2020. MaGraw-Hill. New York.

Neumeier, Marty. *ZAG.* 2007. New Riders. Peachpit Press. Berkeley.

Neumeier, Marty. *The Designful Company.* 2009. New Riders. Peachpit Press. Berkeley.

Neumeier, Marty. *The Brand Gap.* 2006. New Riders. Peachpit Press. Berkeley.

Neumeier, Marty. *The Brand Flip.* 2015. New Riders. Peachpit Press. Berkeley.

Phillips, Peter L. *Creating the Perfect Design Brief: How to Manage Design for Strategic Advantage. Second Edition.* 2004. Allworth Press. New York.

Sandel, Kady. BrandFix: *A Brand strategy guide for Busy Entrepreneurs.* 2019.

Schultz, Mike & Doerr, John E. *Professional Services Marketing: How the best firms build premier brands, thriving lead generation engines and cultures of business development success.* 2009. The Wellesley Hills Group. Hoboken.

Signorelli, Jim. *StoryBranding 2.0.* 2014 Greenleaf Book Group LLC. Austin.

Smith, Lyn. *Effective Internal Communication.* 2008. Kogan Page.

Thornton, Gail, S; Mansk, Viviane Regina; Carramenha, Bruno; Cappelland, Thatiana. *Strategic Employee Communication: Building a Culture of Engagement.* 2018. Springer.

van Riel, Cees B.M. & Fambrun, Charles, J. *Essentials of Corporate Communications.* 2007. Routledge.

Wheeler, Alina. *Designing Brand Identity. Fifth Edition.* 2018. John Wiley & Sons, Inc. Hoboken.

Yohn, Denise Lee. *Fusion: How integrating brand and culture powers the World's Greatest Companies.* 2018. Nicholas Brealey Publishing. Boston.

Yohn, Denise Lee. *What Great Brands Do: The Seven Brand-Building Principles that Separate the Best from the Rest.* 2014. Jossey-Bass. San Francisco.

Websites:

Morton, J. (1997). A guide to color symbolism. COLORCOM. Retrieved on August 14, 2012 from http://www. colorvoodoo.com/cvoodoo1.html

Color Matters. http://www.colormatters. com/

How to Find Your Writing Voice. http:// www.enchantingmarketing.com/how- to-find-your-writing-voice/

Kuler. https://color.adobe.com/

SWOT Analysis. Mindtools. https:// www.mindtools.com/pages/article/ newTMC_05.htm

Understanding Voice and Tone in Writing. http://www.quickanddirtytips. com/education/grammar/ understanding-voice-and-tone-in- writing

Visual Color Symbolism Chart by Culture. http://webdesign.about. com/od/webdesign/fl/Visual-Color-

Symbolism-Chart-by-Culture.htm

https://www.swiftdigital.com.au/blog/
internal-communications-survey/

https://bamboo.com

https://www.lumapps.com/resources/
checklists/checklist-internal-
communication-plan/?creative=

359275095108&keyword=best%20
internal%20communications%20
strategy&-matchtype=p&network=

g&device=c&gclid=EAIaIQobChMIkbCgm
4rc-gIVGvnICh3Adw84EAAYAiAAEgIm6_

D_BwE

INDEX

—— A ——

Accessibility 198

Articles 126, 183, 201, 213

Audience Engagement 203

Audits 199

Authority 11

—— B ——

Behaviors 72, 170, 176

Beliefs 19, 219

Blog Posts 213

Brand Guidelines. *See* Brand Standards

Brand Identity 105

Branding Resonance 20

Brandmark 106, 107, 123

Brand Messaging 187

Brand Positioning 186

Brand Recognition 12, 13

Brand Standards 188, 190

Brand Story 187

Brand Strategy 186

—— C ——

Collaboration 165, 166, 171, 194

Color 105, 111, 112, 113, 114, 115, 121, 122, 126, 127, 187, 188, 189, 229

Brand Color System 114

Color Palette 187, 188

Primary Colors 188

Secondary Colors 188

Tertiary Colors 189

Default Color System 114

Signature Color System 114

Supporting Color System 114

Colors 59, 88, 101, 111, 188, 189. *See* Color

Communication , 40, 99, 133, 134, 138, 139, 143, 144, 149, 165, 171, 175, 187, 200, 205, 207, 210, 211, 221, 224, 229

Communication Style 187

Competitive Analysis 187

Consistency 11, 16, 17, 25, 33, 41, 52, 55, 60, 61, 64, 84, 111, 152, 184, 214

Content Calendar 146, 208, 226

Crisis Management 64, 209, 211

Cues 72, 175

Culture 159

—— D ——

DEI. *See* Diversity, Equity, and Inclusion

Demographics 78, 80, 81, 92, 186, 214, 219, 239

Differentiation 9

Digital Footprint 197

Diversity, Equity, and Inclusion 167

—— E ——

Employee Development 155, 166

Employee Engagement 163

Endorsements 11

Events 183

—— F ——

Feedback 133, 136, 165, 171, 195, 225

Foundations 133, 136

—— G ——

Goals ix, 90, 91, 103, 139, 187, 239

—— I ——

Iconography 189

Identity 187

Imagery 187, 189

Inclusivity. *See* Accessibility

Influencers 204

Infographics 151, 202, 213

Internal Communication Strategy 134, 139

—— K ——

Key Performance Indicators. *See* KPIs

KPIs 140, 141, 187

—— L ——

Legal Compliance 200

Live Sessions 201

Logo 59, 88, 127, 187, 188

Logotype 106, 107

—— M ——

Marketing v, xi, xii, 18, 23, 67, 80, 81, 86, 122, 126, 135, 138, 144, 148, 182, 183, 191, 201, 228, 240

Mission 36, 69, 90, 91, 102, 103, 154, 186

Mission Statement 90, 91. *See* Mission

—— N ——

Nomenclature 108

—— O ——

Organizational Personality 97, 157

—— P ——

Patient Experience 64, 94

Patient Loyalty 13, 14, 15, 20, 21, 29, 64

Perception 7, 15, 63

Personality 45, 51, 97, 98, 133, 134, 157, 187, 189

Personas viii, 78, 186, 241

Positioning 43, 133, 134, 186

Positioning Statement 186

Practice Name 87

Press Releases 183, 240

Promise 33, 45, 133, 134

Psychographics 92, 186, 240

Purpose 35, 36, 67, 72, 133, 134, 160, 161, 213

—— R ——

Recognition 11, 40, 72, 156, 172, 174, 225

Repurpose Content 208

Reputation 11

Rituals 72, 174

  Celebratory Rituals 174

  Communication Rituals 72, 174

  Onboarding Rituals 72, 174

  Recognition Rituals 72, 174

  Social Rituals 72, 174

  Wellness Rituals 72, 174

—— S ——

Signage 122, 126, 183, 192, 240

  External Signage 183

Signature 106, 107, 114, 115, 116, 117, 118, 122, 123, 126, 191

Slogans 187, 240

Social Media 5, 80, 145, 146, 183, 191, 194, 201, 219, 224, 226, 227

Social Proof 11

SOPs x, 184, 185, 240

Standard Operating Procedures. *See* SOPs

Storytelling 57, 60

Strategy 186, 188

Style Guides. *See* Brand Standards

SWOT 89, 90, 92, 187, 229

——— T ———

Tagline 56, 106, 117, 122

Taglines 187

Target Audience 36, 43, 79, 92, 147, 186, 219

Templates 120, 126, 190, 191, 192

  Client-Facing Documents 191

  Digital Assets 191

  Event Materials 192

  Guideline Documents 192

  Internal Communications ix, x, 133, 136, 138, 192

  Marketing Materials 122, 126, 183, 191

  Online Presence 192

  Promotional Merchandise 192

  Stationery Templates 191

  Video And Multimedia 192

Testimonials 11, 202

Tone vii, viii, 55, 60, 143, 185, 187, 189, 229, 241

Tone of Voice 187, 189

Touchpoint *See* Touchpoints

Touchpoints 125, 126, 186, 187

Trustworthiness 10, 11, 20, 33, 190, 193

Typography 60, 119, 122, 126, 187, 189, 220

——— U ———

Unique Selling Propositions 9

Unique Value Proposition. *See* UVP

User Experience 197

User-Generated Content (UGC) 206, 208

User Personas 186

USP *See* Unique Selling Propositions

UVP 186

——— V ———

Values 69, 72, 90, 91, 92, 102, 103, 133, 134, 154, 159, 186, 219

Vision 35, 40, 69, 133, 134, 160, 186, 211

Visual 184, 187

Visual Consistency 17, 184

Visual Identity 187

Voice 41, 47, 55, 99, 101, 122, 157, 187, 189, 211, 229

——— W ———

Webinars 201

Website 23, 121, 126, 183, 187, 192

www.ingramcontent.com/pod-product-compliance
Lightning Source LLC
Chambersburg PA
CBHW061147220326
41599CB00025B/4391